"Simple and profound, this book is a testament to an ethical, and political commitment to the colonized peoples of America."

—Casa de las Américas Prize committee

"When I read *Paletó and Me*, I had a wonderful revelation. Our ancestors, with wisdom and magic, foresaw an irrepressible capacity of people to affect worlds and to make families across cultures. And I gained a 'relative' in the talented writer Aparecida Vilaça, whose anthropology is made of affects between worlds."

—Ailton Krenak, author of
Ideas to Postpone the End of the World

"In this extraordinary account, the rich experiences of a seasoned social anthropologist are superbly sustained by novelistic insights. Aparecida Vilaça takes us on a journey into a profoundly alien culture by entering the mind of one man, Paletó. His life spanned, it seemed, an entire history of human civilization. From an upbringing and early adulthood in an uncontacted tribe in the Amazon forest to the explosive, savage intrusions of modernity, his outlook remained deeply humane. Through him, Vilaça holds up a mirror to the unchanging fundamentals of human nature."

—Ian McEwan

"The wonderful draw of *Paletó and Me* is the courage of one woman immersing herself in another culture and 'making relatives.' Through her acute observations, Aparecida Vilaça conveys a way of being to any reader who may not know how one indigenous community continues to exist."

—Linda Hogan, author of
The Radiant Lives of Animals

"Paletó and Aparecida's unlikely, potent kinship is narrated unforgettably in this book, without the narrator glossing over any of the violence of colonialism across which it happened. Kinship is always a surprise, never to be taken for granted. *Paletó and Me* shows how such a surprise continues to matter."

—Donna Haraway, author of
Staying with the Trouble: Making Kin in the Chthulucene

"In this fascinating account, Aparecida Vilaça at times effaces herself—concealed by her friend's lively voice—and at times reemerges in the luminous form of her singular and personal writing. Far from being a conventional anthropological text, *Paletó and Me* depicts the inebriating journey between identities that reveal themselves to be both ancient and fleeting."

—Mia Couto, author of *Sleepwalking Land*

"Written in a conversational tone and guided by memories, *Paletó and Me* is inspired by questions rather than conclusions and completely forsakes ideology, rendering Aparecida Vilaça's memories into a delightful story."

—Paulo Roberto Pires, *Época Magazine*

PALETÓ AND ME

PALETÓ and ME

MEMORIES OF MY INDIGENOUS FATHER

APARECIDA VILAÇA

Translated by David Rodgers

STANFORD UNIVERSITY PRESS
Stanford, California

STANFORD UNIVERSITY PRESS

Stanford, California

Paletó and Me was originally published in Portuguese in 2018 under the title *Paletó e eu: memórias de meu pai indígena* © 2018, Todavia.

Images are published with permission.

Beto Barcellos: pp. 21, 22, 26, 28, 32, 92, 174

Archives of the Prelacy of Guajará-Mirim: pp. 138, 139

Gilles de Catheu: p. 157

Carlos Fausto: p. 218

All other images by Aparecida Vilaça.

Printed in the United States of America on acid-free, archival-quality paper

Library of Congress Cataloging-in-Publication Data

Names: Vilaça, Aparecida, 1958- author. | Rodgers, David (Translator),translator.

Title: Paletó and me : memories of my Indigenous father / Aparecida Vilaça ; translated by David Rodgers.

Other titles: Paletó e eu. English

Description: Stanford, California : Stanford University Press, 2021. |"Originally published in Portuguese in 2018 under the title Paletó e eu: memórias de meu pai indígena." | Includes bibliographical referencesand index.

Identifiers: LCCN 2021018476 (print) | LCCN 2021018477 (ebook) | ISBN 9781503629332 (paperback) | ISBN 9781503629349 (epub)

Subjects: LCSH: Vilaça, Aparecida, 1958- | Paletó, -2017. | Pakaasnovos Indians—Brazil—Biography. | Women ethnologists—Brazil—Biography.

Classification: LCC F2520.1.P32 V56513 2021 (print) | LCC F2520.1.P32(ebook) | DDC 305.80092 [B]—dc23

LC record available at https://lccn.loc.gov/2021018476

LC ebook record available at https://lccn.loc.gov/2021018477

Cover design: Kevin Barrett Kane

Cover image: Aparecida Vilaça

Text design: Kevin Barrett Kane

Typeset at Stanford University Press in 11/15 ITC Galliard Pro

CONTENTS

CONTENTS

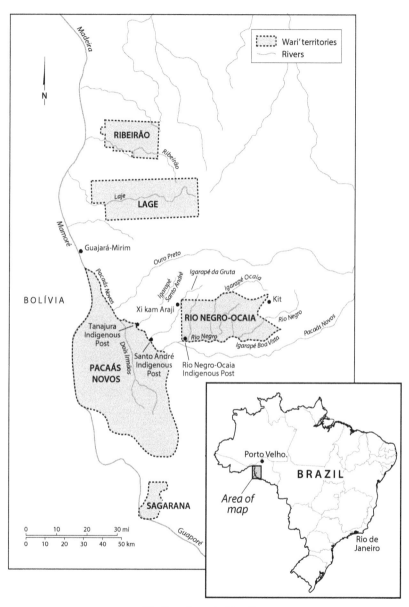

Wari' territory in Brazil

1.

DEATH WITHOUT CANNIBALISM

FROM THE MOMENT I first noticed him aging, I often caught myself wondering whether I would be able to weep over his death in the Wari' way, in which a sung speech celebrating the dead person's life alternates with fits of sobbing. In this song the mourner recalls shared moments, the times spent eating together, how each person cared for the other. Some people, seeing me by his side, and perhaps noticing my tender gaze toward the man who had adopted me as a daughter, thought the same and asked me whether I would be there when he died.

I am not. He died in the interior of Rondônia, in the north of Brazil, and I remain in Rio de Janeiro, trying to imagine his body, the white hairs sprouting from his chin, his strong arms. I vividly remember each of these details, and cannot imagine any part of him lifeless. He moves, he shines, he talks to me.

No matter his age, perhaps over 85, his demise was sudden for me, despite his increasing frailty caused by Parkinson's disease. He had been well, ate sweetcorn with relish, and was able to get out and walk, I was told by his daughter Orowao Karaxu, my elder sister with whom he

lived in his final few months, in the village called Linha
26, about three hundred kilometers from Porto Velho,
the state capital. Apparently, he ate some spoiled meat,
fell sick, became dehydrated, and was taken to the hospital
in the city of Guajará-Mirim by Orowao Karaxu's son-in-
law. Arriving already in a very weakened state, he asked
to phone me, but someone suggested waiting until the
next day when he would be in a better condition to speak.
Paletó went into a coma that night from kidney failure
and died twenty-four hours later in the same hospital. We
never talked again.

That is, I never again heard his voice. I hold on to the
hope that he had heard mine, over the mobile phone that I
asked the doctor, my friend Gilles de Catheu, Gil, to cradle
near his ear. I had no real idea what to say, but what came
to me was to tell him in Wari' (the only language he understood) that I was thinking of him, I missed him, I wanted him
to stay strong, and that my sons, his grandsons, Francisco
and André, were by my side, thinking of him too. Gil told
me that he didn't move and made no sign that he had heard
me, but I hope my voice reached him.

Maybe—I wonder now—he had reached me even before
I had called to reach him. The night he was hospitalized,
when I was still unaware of anything happening, I dreamed
of him. He was young and handsome, strong as always, with
all his teeth. He spoke with the same clarity as before he
became ill. In the dream, I told him I was astonished by his
youthfulness, and he smiled proudly. Perhaps it was already
his double who had come to visit me, in the young form that
inhabits the world of the dead, traditionally situated, for the
Wari', underwater, at the bottom of the rivers—or, since they
had become Evangelicals, in the sky.

I woke up happy from this dream, thinking that now, in January 2017, it had been exactly one year since I had last seen him, and realizing how much I wanted to see him again. But no sooner had I gotten out of bed and looked at my mobile did I find the WhatsApp message from Preta, a Funai (National Indian Foundation)* employee and longtime friend, telling me that sadly Paletó was very ill in hospital. It was then that the many calls and messages began, with detailed news on his state of health.

I received one photo showing him lying on a mattress that was covered in blue plastic. His head was resting on rolled-up cloths and he was covered in a red, patterned blanket, under which his legs appeared spread out, knees apart and feet close together, just the way he liked to sleep. Because he was not wearing his dentures, his lips were sunken. "He doesn't like being without his dentures!" I thought. I was later told by the nurse that they had been removed to prevent him from choking on them. Later, when discussing the burial by telephone, I asked for them to be put back in. I hope they were.

After seeing the photo, I received information that I couldn't decipher but that unnerved me, so I called a doctor friend in Rio. I wanted to know what "extremely high" levels of urea and creatinine might signify. Other information was more comprehensible but no less unsettling, such as the fact that he had only urinated fifty millimeters in twenty-four hours and, moreover, that the urine had contained blood. Then, when I talked with Gil, he summed up the clinical

* The National Indian Foundation (Funai) was created in 1967 to replace the Indian Protection Service (SPI). Both are government agencies designed to deal with all Indigenous affairs in Brazil, including contact policies and lands protection.

situation: Paletó was in a coma. But his pulse was strong, he added. I knew that Paletó would fight. He had already survived many wars and various epidemics, seen so many people fall ill and die around him, that one day, on my last visit to him, at the end of 2015, he told me that I shouldn't worry about his health because he "didn't know how to die." After talking with Gil, I called the hospital nurses, who gave me more detailed news, including that a hemodialysis had been recommended at one point, but then quickly discounted since it would require a journey to Porto Velho, which would have meant about four hours in an ambulance. Distraught and separated by almost four thousand kilometers, I still tried to convince people, including my sisters, to consider this intervention, perhaps his only chance for survival. Orowao, the eldest, had her doubts, while Ja, the youngest, was vehement: "We're not going to take him." She was right, since she would be the one by his side some hours later when, emerging from the coma, he sat up in bed, called for his daughter Orowao, lay down again and died. According to Ja, at three in the morning. According to Julião, Orowao's son-in-law, at five.

It was the message sent by Julião that I received on awakening at seven: Paletó had died. So difficult to believe. And it still is today, a day later, as I begin to write this account. I can only imagine him alive, as vividly alive as he ever was. Julião's mobile phone took me to my younger sister, Ja, who then placed me in the middle of the funeral song, so well known to me but bewilderingly strange now that I found myself impelled to take part as a daughter. Ja was singing and sobbing. In her song she called me Apa or older sister. She sang that she couldn't bear such suffering: our mother had died in August with her head in Ja's lap, in a canoe in

4

the middle of the river, and now we had lost our father. She asked me to come, but soon agreed with me that I wouldn't be able to arrive in time, before his body was buried.

As I had feared when imagining that moment, the tears ran down by face but I couldn't sing. Overwhelmed, I was unable to repeat the melody expected of me, or speak through the song. All I could manage to say, repeating myself endlessly, was that we had lost our father and that everything in our home in Rio reminded me of him, a place full of memories from his visits, when he taught me many things, told me his life story, and was continually surprised by and curious about what he saw in this big city, where everything seemed so strange to him. "Don't people here sleep?" he asked one day after noticing that the lights in the streets and in some of the buildings never went out. "How is a place without shadows possible?" he pondered when visiting an exhibition at the Moreira Salles Institute, where the lighting was designed to cast no shadows. "He's going to die and you aren't worried!" he exclaimed on seeing for the first time my stepson Gabriel surf in Barra.

I continued with Ja, my younger sister, on the phone. Singing, she asked me for food for the boys who were arriving for the wake. Singing, she told me about the death of our mother a few months earlier. Clinging to the mobile, I could only repeat myself, feeling so frustrated at being unable to sing. She then let me go, ending the call so that I could phone Gil, my doctor friend, to ask him to take food, which he did right away. He took coffee and bread to the port on the Mamoré River, where they cried, hugging the coffin. "Nobody touched the food," he told me afterward. You don't eat while you are crying.

Lying down, staring up at my bedroom ceiling, I fretted about not being there. And then I thought of something that might make Paletó happy, were he somehow able to witness the scene. I called the funeral home and asked them to place him in a beautiful padded coffin, dress him in a smart shirt and trousers, and put on polished shoes with laces. I wanted people, not just his family, to look upon him as someone special, to see him as the important man that he was, so wise, strong, good-humored, curious, open. An adult who never lost the best of himself as a child, despite seeing so many sad things, including several of his close kin shot and killed by rubber tappers sixty years earlier. I once asked him if he didn't hate White people because of these episodes, all of us White people, and he, kind as always, replied that my family and I had nothing to do with what these Whites had done. I am grateful for his forgiveness.

Larissa, a nurse, and Jôice, a social assistant, there in distant Guajará, went to the funeral home. They asked for the coffin to be changed and told me that they had dressed him as I had requested, save for the shoes. There were none available: the dead at the funeral home wore only socks. "It's not possible," I said. "He has to go with nice shoes!" In the Christian heaven, where for some years Paletó had counted on going, everyone is young, beautiful, and well dressed, and most particularly, everyone wears shoes, the rarest item in the Wari' wardrobe. "Does he wear size nine and a half?" Jôice asked. "Yes," I responded, but then I remembered that his toes splay out a lot, and perhaps his feet were also swollen. "No, get ten and a halfs." "Bought them!" she told me via WhatsApp.

The temperature in Rio de Janeiro on this January 10, 2017, is unbearable and I imagine the heat in Rondônia and the voyage that Paletó will have to make to the Negro River and the village of Ocaia III, where his house sits and where most of his children live. Jôice phoned from the funeral home to say that he was all sorted. With the fine padded coffin came a kind of VIP service that included embalming and a wreath of flowers. She took a photo to show me, but I asked her not to send it. I wanted to hold on to the memory of his young double who had appeared to me in the dream the night before.

A short while later I received a message from Preta, now with an attached photo of the closed coffin taken at a distance, showing people laying across it, crying. I recognized my sister Orowao leaning on a nearby wall, looking exhausted, and my sister Ja hugging the coffin. A scene of unbearable sorrow. I noticed a cloth draped over the casket and zoomed in on the photo to see what appeared to be the flag of a soccer team, white and green. I asked my son André, who was by my side and knows everything about soccer, which team it was; he immediately replied, "Palmeiras." I was confused. Paletó had never shown any interest in the sport and his son Abrão, as far as I know, is a Vasco fan. But Palmeiras had been Brazilian champions in 2016: Had they wanted to give Paletó the sendoff of a champion?

I was told that the *voadeira* (a small boat with a forty-horsepower outboard motor) left the port at 10:30, the sun already high in the sky. I imagine the journey, the stops in the various villages en route for relatives to be able to see the deceased, the dramatic arrival at the destination with a crowd of people waiting and crying, including three of his children—Abrão, Davi, and Main, who had decided not to go to the hospital. They will spend the night crying, now with the casket open and the body able to be touched and embraced. Perhaps they will take the body out of the coffin and lay it on the floor. Then someone will lie down on the floor and slide themselves under the body, and others will follow, each lying under the previous person, forming a human pile that is maintained until the last person faints and is removed. They want the smells, the liquids, everything that the body can still offer them.

In the past, when an important man died, who had himself taken part in many festivals, the body would be carried on the shoulders of a living man and offered sweetcorn *chicha*, a fermented, alcoholic drink, just as one offers to guests during a festival. Soon after, his double would arrive in the subaquatic world of the dead, where he would drink more chicha, offered by a man with big testicles called Towira Towira ("Testicle Testicle"). Full of chicha, the double would vomit and then be taken to the men's house for a period of seclusion, in the same way as a warrior after a successful war expedition. And indeed, for the Wari', the dead man had turned into a warrior, hence his young and vigorous appearance—like the double of Paletó who had appeared in my dream.

In the past, the dead were not buried, as Paletó will be in his coffin in the cemetery upriver. The burial site was established by the US Evangelical missionaries of the New Tribes Mission, who arrived in the region of the Negro River in 1961 to help in what was euphemistically referred to as the "pacification" of the Wari'. Missionaries remain in some of the villages to this day. In the past, Paletó's body would have been free of the coffin, placed on the stilt palm platform, held by kin, while other people prepared the fire that would roast it. Two or three days would pass until everyone arrived from other villages to see the body still intact, to hug it and place themselves under it. Some of the closest kin, driven to despair by the death and with everyone around them distracted, would suddenly throw themselves on the fire, wanting to join the loved one in the underwater world where all people eventually go. Usually they were rescued and survived; some, however, died.

I recall Paletó often dramatizing for me the various movements related to the dead person and to those mourning the death, so that I could understand the ceremony and record and film the stages of its enactment. On one occasion, Paletó, Abrão, and I were in the living room of my apartment in Rio de Janeiro. Two chairs, joined by broom handles, functioned as the funeral grill. A wadded newspaper underneath was the bonfire. A cheap plastic doll with detachable legs, arms, and head, bought by us at a downtown store, was the dead person.

Paletó insisted that I take an active part, instead of only filming, so I could learn the details of the ritual properly. He demonstrated the roles of the two groups involved in the funeral: as kin to the deceased, I should cry, walk around crouching and singing (You see? I had even rehearsed the song that I was unable to sing at the necessary moment!) and asking non-kin, one by one, to eat the deceased. When performing the role of non-kin, he taught me to take the roasted flesh, which was divided into small pieces (substituted there by bread) and, using chopsticks, place each piece in my mouth delicately, showing gentleness to the kin of the dead person who had asked me to make the body disappear by eating it.

The dead person's kin asked others to eat the body to complete its disappearance, as its sight provoked intense longing and sadness. The kin themselves, overwhelmed by the physical presence of the deceased, which left the person still alive in their memory, were incapable of doing so. But it was not just the body's disappearance that the Wari' sought when asking that others eat pieces of the flesh of their dead kin; simply burning the corpse would have achieved the same objective. By eating the body, non-kin showed to the mourners that a corpse is no longer a person and thus can be eaten. Hence, they initiated the lengthy process of mourning on the part of kin, which would culminate in their own eventual capacity to adopt the perspective of non-kin, the eaters, eliminating from their memory the human embodiment of the deceased.

In our enactment, Abrão and I took turns performing the roles of those who cry and those who eat, and also, in this case, those who film. Abrão quickly learned to handle the camera, and the stability of the image was only lost when the three of us fell into fits of laughter, one time right at the moment when Paletó tried to throw himself in the fire-newspaper and Abrão needed to rescue him.

Paletó told me more than once that he found it difficult to eat the flesh of people, which usually had a very strong smell, better described as a stench. He told me how a dead woman's kin once asked him, while still a young man, to eat her flesh. Paletó said that he tried, eating a small amount, but soon afterward quietly sneaked away to vomit. I assumed, since it was the corpse of an adult woman, it must have been far along in the process of decay, as they would have waited days for the arrival of all her kin before cutting up and roasting the body.

Paletó spoke a lot about this during our filming and, in one of the scenes where I feigned eating the flesh of the dead doll, he made me turn aside and pretend to vomit. He explained that this should never be done in front of the deceased's kin, as it would be considered indelicate. But what was really indelicate, he added, was eating the flesh with the same relish that one eats game. Immediately after death, the corpse is still not animal and, though this is what it will turn into later, it was important to respect the perspective of kin, who still saw the body as a person, as though alive, in the same way that I now see Paletó in my memories. The risk of such a faux pas—eating flesh with a display of pleasure—was greater when the flesh was roasted before it became rotten, as in the case of a dead child, whose wake was shorter.

In the past, everything was eaten. The body was consumed entirely, leaving nothing of the dead person's flesh. If by chance something was left, it was thrown on the fire along with the bones, all to be burned and thus to vanish. All of the deceased's belongings were also burned, as well as their house, the plants of their garden, even the tree trunks where the person had sat along the forest paths. The Wari' called this act of destruction "sweeping"—sweeping up everything of the dead person, which included shaving off the hair of close kin, frequently touched fondly by the deceased.

Paletó once told me that were I to die, he would cry profusely. He would rip up the clothes that I had given him and throw them on the fire. I think about what they will do today with Paletó's belongings, among them his suitcase, always with him, his clothes, the red scarf I gave him some years ago, blankets, shorts. Will they destroy them? Will they give them away? Or sell them to someone, as they tend to do today with more durable items like radios or televisions? To'o Xak Wa, his wife, once told me that in the past this was never an issue, since the only durable items were clay pots, which would be smashed and thrown on the fire that roasted the deceased.

Paletó no longer had many possessions, since he lived—in the company of his wife, until she died—with one son or another who looked after their parents and fed them. In the last few years, he had become increasingly frail as a result of Parkinson's disease. He often said that he became weak after falling in the water while fishing alone in a canoe one day. Not knowing how to swim, he almost drowned and was rescued, unconscious, by one of his sons. After that he trembled a lot, as though the cold of the water had inextricably infiltrated his body.

I look at photos on my computer, taken in 2015 when I last saw him. He's singing and laughing, but with his eyes almost always closed. What didn't he want to see? This man lived for at least thirty years in the forest, without contact with White people, save for the war raids, and unfamiliar with any of the items of our civilization, apart from metal tools, which they obtained from empty rubber-tapper houses. He had seen the arrival of White people, their new diseases, their strange food and clothing. People say that after refusing to cover himself with what they offered him, he finally became smitten with a jacket, a "paletó" in Portuguese, and began to wear it over his otherwise naked body. That was when he, who had been called Watakao', became known as Paletó. With his jacket he traveled to other villages and visited the town of Guajará-Mirim. He arrived in Rio de Janeiro, discovered the telephone and the internet, and I see him now, in a photo on my wall panel, speaking with me on Skype when he was in Guajará-Mirim, in the house of Gil, who photographed him. Did closing his eyes allow him to return to these images of the past? Sometimes he would recall something from one of his visits to Rio and recount it to me, laughing, such as the hippopotamus he saw at the zoo: why didn't we eat these animals, or the pigeons that flocked in the squares, or the monkeys roaming in Tijuca Forest? He was surprised when I gave my son raw fish to eat in a Japanese restaurant: wasn't I afraid that he'd be eaten by a jaguar that would smell the blood? "But there aren't any jaguars here in the city, Dad!" "Ah, but what about those enormous dogs? Do you really think they can't sniff out blood?"

As they did in the past, my kin, there on the Negro River, will stay in mourning for a long time, crying and singing the funeral melody every day and, through it, remembering the acts of the deceased, Paletó, the care and food he gave to his family. They will eat almost nothing, their bodies becoming thinner and their voices hoarse. In the past, after months had gone by, a close family member would decide to end the mourning, inviting everyone to a hunt lasting a few days. They would return carrying baskets filled with dead animals, already roasted, and enter the village at the same time of day as the person's death. They would put the baskets down and cry around them, in the same way as they cried for the dead, singing the funeral melody and remembering the person's feats, as well as the small acts of care shown to them. They would cry not only for the recently dead person but for others too, those who were still remembered. And then everyone would eat the roasted game, finally able to laugh and referring to the meat as "corpse." "Do you want a bit of corpse?" someone would say, tearing off a chunk carelessly, without chopsticks, to offer to someone else. It was a corpse but also, now at last, game. A transformation had occurred and so they celebrated. The deceased, eaten as game, temporarily left the world of the living and people's memory.

Paletó will not be eaten. Perhaps he would have wanted to be, since the Wari' were traditionally horrified by burial, the idea that the body would linger under the earth for a long time. But I know Paletó also feared that, without a whole body, he would not be resurrected and allowed into heaven to live near to God. In 2001, amid the Christian revivalism that followed the attack on the World Trade Center, an event they had seen unfold on the community television and which provoked fears of the imminent end of the world, Paletó along with many other people had reconverted to the Christianity of the missionaries. He no longer wanted to go to the subaquatic world but rather to heaven, where all the others who had died as Christians would be waiting.

Today I would very much like this heaven, where he longed to go, to exist, just to welcome Paletó, well dressed as he was in his laced shoes. On arrival he would certainly be admired by everyone; and who knows, perhaps by God himself, who—although never appearing to those in heaven, according to the Wari'—might make an exception and see him arrive.

2.
THE ENCOUNTER

I WAS INTRODUCED to Paletó by his son Abrão, then aged eighteen. I met Abrão for the first time the day after my arrival in 1986 at the Rio Negro-Ocaia Post, a Wari' village situated close to the mouth of the Negro River, an affluent of the Pacaás Novos, itself an affluent of the Mamoré, in the state of Rondônia. I had arrived with my entire kit and caboodle, ready to stay for months doing field research, an essential part of the initiation of any anthropologist. In Rio, I had left behind my family, my boyfriend, and my work as a biologist (yes, I was a biologist, trained in plant ecology!) and, lugging two large bags and a folding chair (my friend Márcio said it was essential to have somewhere comfortable to sit), set out on a nine-hour flight destined for Porto Velho—and many connections en route. Later, in the taxi to the hotel that had been recommended by another anthropologist friend who knew the city, I surprised myself with my reply to the driver's question: "Are you moving here?" Yes, I was.

At night, Porto Velho had the look of an abandoned Wild West town, and no less did my room, where cockroaches scuttled about unperturbed. I spent most of the time awake, wondering what I had gotten myself into. After all, I already had a job that allowed me to live independently in a nice apartment in the bohemian neighborhood of Santa Teresa. And yet here I was in Porto Velho, my head full of dreams and anthropological theories, and books by Carlos Castañeda, in search of my own shaman Don Juan.

As the saying goes, "tomorrow is another day." I awoke freshly determined, ready to organize my flight to Guajará-Mirim, where I would meet an American anthropologist with whom I had been corresponding for months, Beth Conklin. I remember this journey all too clearly since I almost died of fright, especially after catching sight of the pilot, who flew the twin-engine plane while grappling an enormous hamburger in one hand, mayonnaise slowly dribbling out of the bun and down his arm. That was the first and last time I made that flight. My anxiety and doubt only began to diminish when I arrived at the house that Beth rented in town. It was very simple, made of timber, but with a familiar hippie air that immediately reminded me of my own apartment back in Santa Teresa.

Beth and I hit it off from the start, so well that years later we became co-godmothers, she of my first son and I of hers. We came from different countries, but we were of the same subculture with our long hair and colorfully patterned Indian skirts. I recall that, as was common in the town of Guajará-Mirim in those days, the house often ran out of water and we had to fill buckets from the river that flowed a few blocks away. There were almost daily outages—at that time, before the town was connected to the power grid, electricity was produced by large municipal generators or, in the house of wealthier residents, by private generators. Inter-urban calls were only possible at a telephone exchange where you entered a cubicle, asked the operator to dial the number, and then waited, knowing full well that your conversation would be overheard by everyone there. Beth would ferry me around by bicycle; I sat on the pillion, a kind of cushioned saddle, with both legs to one side, just like the local women.

Beth's kindness was such that, realizing I was apprehensive, she offered to travel with me to the Negro River and introduce me to some people she knew. On the way back, she would stay at Santo André village, some two or three hours downriver, where she did fieldwork. On the eve of departure, while we were chatting, I had chosen the Rio Negro-Ocaia Post after learning from her it that was the Wari' village farthest from the town, one of the largest (around three hundred people) and also the most beautiful.

It was not only the choice of the Negro-Ocaia that I had made on the spur of the moment: my decision to study the Wari' had also been, in a certain sense, random, even though more than once during their Sunday services in recent years I have heard the Wari' say that God had guided me to them. The earthbound explanation for my path to the Wari' was, however, as follows. My colleagues and I, master's and doctoral students in social anthropology at the Museu Nacional, all supervised by Eduardo Viveiros de Castro, were huddled around a map of Brazil, studying the locations of Indigenous peoples, and paying special attention to a region of Amazonia still little researched at the time. One of these colleagues, Márcio Silva—the same Márcio who would later recommend I take a folding chair—remarked that he had spent a few months working as a linguist among the Wari' of Sagarana village, founded by Catholic priests on the Guaporé River, and that he had found them very friendly. I decided that very instant. It was just what I needed to hear, since a few months earlier I had heard a desperate account from a friend who had accompanied an anthropologist during the latter's stay with another Indigenous group where, according to her, bad tempers abounded.

Waiting for us the next day at the port was the pilot from the National Indian Foundation (Funai), Francisco das Chagas, "Chaguinha," who has accompanied me over these thirty years of river journeys. A strong man, talkative and cheerful, he is also a highly skilled pilot who knows every small meander of the region's waterways. Whenever I get into the boat with him, I know my journey will be serene and incident-free. I'll never forget when Chagas, in 1993, with a broken arm in a plaster cast, went to fetch me, my then-husband Beto and my son Francisco, just two years old at the time, on the Negro River as soon as we learned via radio that our apartment in Laranjeiras had been burgled and nearly cleared out. After such kindness, I managed to obtain an official shirt of his soccer team, Vasco, signed by the players, which he placed in a glass frame and hung up on the wooden wall of his house.

On that first trip, after filling the aluminum canoe, fitted with an outboard motor, with our bags and boxes of supplies (powdered milk, rice, cooking oil, beans, lentils, salt, sugar, biscuits, instant coffee, guava paste, condensed milk) bought at the local market, Beth and I settled onto one of the seats and we set off. At that time, wearing life jackets wasn't compulsory. Chagas took up his station in the stern next to the motor, and between him and us sat a fifty-liter barrel of gasoline, needed for the return journey, which we used as a backrest.

The landscape of this boat journey to the Negro River, which, depending on the power of the outboard motor, can last up to nine hours, still leaves me spellbound. I used to amplify this sensation by listening to music on my headphones throughout the journey—everything from Caetano Veloso, Gilberto Gil, and the Tribalistas to Jimi Hendrix and Janis Joplin. After traveling up a small section of the Mamoré with its muddy waters, as Bolivia rolled by on the other shore, we entered the Pacaás Novos with its waters the color of tea, the same tint as its affluent, the Negro. Much narrower than the Mamoré, both shores of the Pacaás Novos, with their exuberant forest vegetation, were clearly visible. Flocks of birds circulated above us the whole time: herons, curassows, macaws, toucans, and parrots. I remember the first impact of these images and sounds, which made me forget my fears from the previous days.

That evening, I wrote my first impression of the voyage on the opening page of my notebook:

We left Guajará at ten in the morning in a Funai boat with a 25 hp outboard motor. Close to midday we were at Tanajura, the first post on the Pacaás Novos River. The Indigenous area is located on the left shore of the river. The village is situated high on a bank and the houses of the missionaries appear first, timber-framed, with curtains. Next come the Wari' houses, which are like those of the ribeirinhos [river-dwelling non-Indigenous population], built on stilts with walls and floor made from paxiúba [a palm tree] and a thatched roof, fronted by a large veranda. I met some Wari' from there and they asked me where I came from. When I said Rio de Janeiro, they immediately asked me about the Maracanã [soccer stadium]. We resumed our journey along the Pacaás Novos river and around 2:30 pm arrived at Santo André post. The same scene, houses raised on paxiúba stilts. They sleep on the paxiúba floor. Beth left her things there and we continued traveling upstream to the Negro River. We entered the river at five in the afternoon. The landscape is different. The river is much narrower and more beautiful. In fifteen minutes, we were at the village. A lot of people were waiting for us on the bank, women, men and children. Edna, the teacher, and Valdir, Funai's chief at the post, also came to greet us. We went directly to Edna's house. In the village, the Funai houses are right in front of the river: Funai's chief, nurse, teacher, and the toolshed. Lots of mango, cashew, and rose apple trees. The Wari' houses spread out to either side and to the rear, all around the soccer pitch. Tracks connect them. The forest surrounds the village. A woman placed a mat on the ground, in front of the house, and picked lice from her husband. (Rio Negro, 8/14/1986)

At the time of my arrival, I was twenty-eight years old, ten years older than Abrão, though we seemed to be almost the same age. We were both young and, at his initiative, we began chatting in the doorway to the teacher's house, Edna, a friendly woman from the Brazilian state of Pará, who hosted me in her brick house with its two bedrooms and kitchen, adjoined to the classroom. Abrão, skinny but strong, with dark, short-cropped hair and a beautiful smile, came up to me and asked for a cigarette. I offered him tobacco and rolling paper, and we began talking in

Portuguese, a language that Abrão already knew, which is why he became my translator in these early years. He asked my name, where I came from, and what my husband's name was. He taught me to say some of my first phrases in Wari': *Aparecida ina ta* (I am Aparecida); *narima nukun wijam ina ta* (I am married to the enemy), the latter being something, I soon discovered, that I should not say publicly, since it confirmed my position as an enemy—which was how the Wari' classified all non-Wari' then, both other Indigenous peoples and those they called *civilizados.* As a joke, the Wari' often asked me to repeat the phrase, in a loud voice, and everyone laughed. Then they asked me to say *Hon ina* (I farted) and laughed even more.

Wandering around the houses with Beth, I was introduced to a family who had lived in Santo André and whom she knew well: Xatoji, her daughter Topa', the latter's husband,

Paletó, me, and Abrão, 1987

Maxun Hat, and his parents, Wan e' and Orowao Xik Waje, who lived in the house right next to theirs. This extended family immediately adopted me. Xatoji must have been in her early forties, at most, and was—something rare among the Wari'—separated from her husband, the father of her two daughters, Topa' and Pijim. Her ex-husband also lived on the Negro-Ocaia, married to Paletó's eldest daughter, Orowao Karaxu. Xatoji never married again and lived at that time in the house of one daughter or the other, sleeping alone in her mosquito net or with a granddaughter.

On my second day there, Xatoji invited me to help her peel manioc, which had been left for a day submerged in the river, close to the bank. Once peeled, it would be squeezed in a basket, sifted, toasted on the fire, and transformed into flour. As we worked, she taught me some words and, perhaps a bit crestfallen by my apparent slow progress, explained that if I wanted to learn the language quickly, I should marry a Wari' man and eat local foods, especially insect larvae roasted in leaves. She concluded in Portuguese: "Do you want to eat critter?"

Adults in general took my desire to learn the language so seriously that a few days after my arrival, I was surprised by a discussion in Wari' between the elder Wan e' (who must have been a little over sixty, nearly my age as I write this) and Hilda, a woman who talked with me in Portuguese. When I asked what they were discussing, she explained: "He said we should speak only in the *gíria* [slang, the word used by the regional population to refer to the native language] with you." Language is necessarily learned by living together. When Beto came to visit me there for the first time, in January 1987, they were surprised he didn't know how to speak the Wari' language like I did, since we had been living together in the two-month interval between my first trip and the second. They would ask me: "Don't you feel sorry for him not knowing how to speak?"

Except for marrying a Wari' man, I followed all of their instructions for learning the language, including the noting down of words and phrases, which I then used to communicate. Eating local foods was always a great pleasure because, at that time, they were delicious: cornbread, unfermented *chicha* (a corn drink), several kinds of fish and roast game. The Wari' relish grubs, insects in their larval phase that live in tree trunks, especially in fallen logs left after clearing their gardens. Because of the look of disgust White people made at the sight of this food, they began to eat them discreetly, while at the same time valuing the larvae as a distinctive element of their diet. At various times they told me that to be Wari', I should eat grubs. However, the opportunity didn't present itself until I had been there almost a month, when I went to the garden of Xatoji, Topa', and Maxun Hat to help plant corn. Juliana, the couple's daughter, then six years old, found one of these grubs, which they call *orojat*, white, very plump, with a head shaped like a little red ball, and brought it to me to eat on the spot, raw and squirming. Without hesitating, in the fearless bloom of my twenty-eight years, and with a huge desire to be accepted by them, I stuffed the still wriggling larva in my mouth, chewed, and swallowed. To my surprise, my initial disgust evaporated almost immediately—the taste of the grub reminded me of an olive. Their approval puffed me with pride, even more so when they shouted out on our return to the village, for everyone to hear, that I had become completely Wari'.

Since then they have always offered me grubs, usually roasted in palm leaves—and eaten that way, they do indeed taste delicious. Headlice, though, which they pick from each other's hair and nibble on, and which they also consider a typical part of their diet, were another thing altogether. Now that they had seen me eat grubs, they tried to persuade me that eating lice would make me even more completely Wari'. I waited a few months to have my own, since eating other people's lice seemed a bit too much. The first one I found on my head I popped straight into my mouth, witnessed by those near to me. Having eaten the insect—so small that I could not really taste anything, but still leaving me with no desire to ever eat one again—I got around the problem thereafter by saying that, having tried lice, I felt that eating them was pointless because they didn't fill your belly. That

became my automatic response to each new attempt to convince me otherwise.

At that time, the Wari' seldom ate rice, beans, and pasta or drank soda, which they now do almost daily, bought with money from government family allowances, pensions, and the wages of Wari' teachers and healthcare agents. I remember the precise moment when I experienced this change, in July 2001, hosted in Paletó's house in Boca village, today called Ocaia III. They generously offered me dishes filled with rice, beans, and pasta, cooked with lots of soybean oil, which I found difficult to eat. A persistent upset stomach led me to stick to a diet of bananas and eggs throughout that stay, and on subsequent trips I brought brown rice, lentils, oats, milk, and biscuits for myself. Cornbread has become a rarity because corn is rarely planted there anymore. The deep pounding of wood on stone while grinding maize, which

used to be a constant soundtrack, is no longer heard. Fish and especially game have become rare.

The day after our first encounter, Abrão sent his sister Ja to my house, then six years old, smart, talkative, and articulate, shoeless and wearing only shorts. In her hands she carried a large piece of surubim catfish to offer me in his name. I asked Ja if Abrão wanted something. Yes, tobacco and rolling paper, she replied. Wanting to appear generous and unaware of the local etiquette not to refuse food, I told her to keep the fish because I would give him what he had asked for anyway. Disconcerted, the girl returned home, and at her reaction I immediately began to wonder if I had acted improperly. Would Abrão be upset by my refusal? Soon enough he appeared at my house and I explained to him that I hadn't accepted the fish because I had already eaten well that day. It was salted, Abrão told me, meaning that I could have kept it for another day.

I had not yet met Paletó, although his name already appeared in my notebooks among a list of older people to meet. According to these notes, on my fourth day, I went to the house of his daughter Orowao Karaxu, and I saw him for the first time, sitting next to his wife, To'o Xak Wa. He asked me questions I didn't understand, and laughed at my quizzical looks in response. His son-in-law, married to Orowao Karaxu, was able to translate some of them for me, such as whether my husband was old, whether my parents were old. Abrão asked for a Flamengo soccer jersey and said that he would like to spend a year in Rio de Janeiro. We had little idea that he would, indeed, come to visit me in Rio various times. I visited Paletó in his house two days later. On that occasion, with Abrão as intermediary, he told me a myth and then sang songs of the Orotapan, a mythic people who live under the water, songs that were accompanied by his wife and recorded by me. They asked me to tell them a story and the first that came to mind was Cinderella, translated for them by Abrão.

My tape recorder was a complete success. Almost every night, women and girls would gather on the patio of Topa' Jam's house and sing for me so I could record them. Afterwards they asked me to play the tape back multiple times. Topa' Jam's house was a lively house, situated on the edge of the slope that went down to the river. Topa' Jam had many daughters, among them Rute, who, along with Dina, her neighbor and the daughter of Wan e', both around twelve years old, became my inseparable companions during those

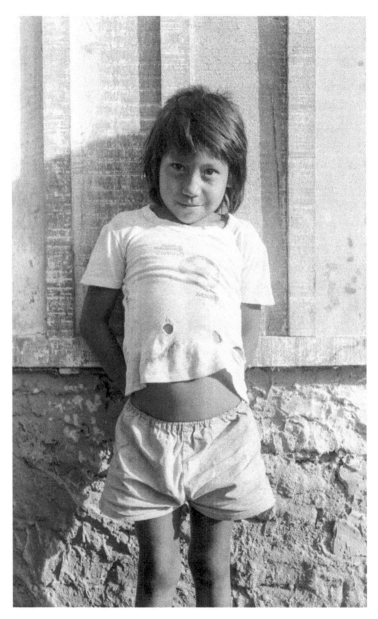

Ja, 1987

first years. Topa' Jam's mother was the oldest woman of the village, the only one with white hair. She was a widow and lived with her daughter, son-in-law, and grandchildren, sharing the work of raising the children and enjoying their daily company.

Gathered on that patio, sitting on mats, men and women listened to the recorded songs repeatedly, but also paid close attention to the background sounds of the young men moving about and joking among themselves and with the female singers. The tape machine was also a way for those not present at the recording to know what was happening in other homes, and what other people had said to me. Through the new technology they amplified their communication networks.

It was on a boat trip two months after my arrival that I called Paletó father for the first time. It was one of the few times I traveled on the large wooden boat of the Funai post, a *chata* (flat) as it is known regionally, which the Wari' called *tonton* (an onomatopoeia derived from the metallic sound of the motor). Many of us were heading downriver to Tanajura village for a festival. It took an eternity to set off because each time we prepared to embark it was announced that someone or something was still missing. I walked the path between my house and the river several times, listening for the announcement that the boat was truly leaving. The journey, when it finally got underway, was supposed to take eight hours at most, but ended up taking two days. My scant provisions were a rucksack containing all my things and a small basket with some cooked sweet manioc and boiled eggs. I thought the food would be enough for the trip and had shared it out among those who asked—it was gone in the first few hours.

When we were close to our destination, by now very hungry and with everyone's food eaten, the passengers decided to stop and fish. I stayed in the boat, accompanied by some young men who were feeling too lazy to take part. One of them, Luís, Paletó's nephew, lay down on the boat's deck with the radio glued to his ear, tuning into the Rádio Nacional de Porto Velho. I found it funny to hear the advertisement for a carpet and silverware store as we sat in that spot, surrounded by forest. Luís switched stations, pausing at a slow song by Roberto Carlos, which he didn't like either. He turned the dial again and found some lively music in which the singer sang about being unable to "live without you." Luís liked it and we listened.

The other Wari' spread out along the river shore. As they caught fish, small fires were made to cook them. Nobody invited me to eat and, unsure what to do, I told Abrão that I was very hungry. He then advised me: "You have to go to our father and ask for food, tell him that you're hungry." I approached Paletó, who sat next to a grill with fish, and, ashamed at finding myself in this fragile position, unusual for me, said exactly what Abrão had suggested: "I'm hungry, father."

I haven't forgotten his reaction, happy to share the fish with me, perhaps pleased with my progress in understanding human relations and activating kinship bonds. It seems it was an explicit lesson. The Wari' are not in the least bit avaricious, always offering whatever they are eating when someone arrives home. And the offer having been made, the recipients are not shy. Years later, during a stay with Paletó and To'o in Sagarana, the village founded by priests on the Guaporé River, we arrived at the house of one of

To'o's distant relatives while they were eating fish. They asked To'o and Paletó if they had eaten, to which they replied no. The owners of the house then offered them fish, which they readily accepted, and soon after offered another, which they again accepted, despite it being evident that there wasn't an abundance in that house.

I am now trying to recall Paletó's face in those first months, but it merges with how he looked at other times when we lived together. I remember the angles of his face, the absence of eyebrows and eyelashes, plucked throughout his life with tweezers made from a twig split down the middle, his broad nose, his hair cut to the height of his ears, parted in the middle and still completely black, and the half-dozen hairs on his chin, also carefully plucked out regularly, which turned white over time. The Wari' detest facial and body hair, including around the genitals, and spouses were always ready to pluck these hairs when they had some spare time together. They said that hairy people looked like animals and regarded the bearded Brazilians encountered in the city as horrendous.

Although Paletó was much shorter than me—his head reached slightly higher than my shoulder—I always had the sensation, both with him and with other Wari' adults, that I saw them from below, perhaps because I felt somewhat child-like when next to them. Paletó was thin but with well-defined muscles on his arms and legs, like those of his son Abrão. But what I remember most vividly are the gestures, the way he moved his arms as he spoke, pointing here and there, and his voice, deep and always soft, as is common among the Wari', for whom speaking loudly is considered aggressive. One of my first memories of him was his involvement in the music

rehearsals for a *tamara* festival in another village. Paletó, I wrote in my diary, acted as a "prompter," crouching in front of the line of singers, whispering the song lyrics to them. A few days later when we were at the actual festival, the Wari' singers danced arm in arm, forming a long line in front of their hosts, who kept up a lively, bantering commentary and offered them maize chicha. Paletó now placed himself behind the line, whispering the lyrics each time they took a step back.

Searching for a photo of him from this period in my first book about the Wari', I'm surprised to discover that it's actually the very first in the book, followed by a photo of Abrão. In this picture, Paletó is squatting with a broad smile on his face, showing his five lower teeth, the only ones he had left at that time, before having them all extracted. He is wearing a soccer shirt, maybe Fluminense, São Paulo, or Grêmio, my son André says, unable to identify it with precision in

the black and white photo. I note now this recurrence of
the soccer team emblems in my pictures of him: in the first
photo of the book, and in the last picture I have of him, the
photo of his coffin, sent to me via WhatsApp.

3.
THE PECCARY BROTHER

A T FIRST, my encounters with Paletó were infrequent.
Wan e' and his family were my first friends in the Negro-
Ocaia River village and they lived in different parts of the
village. Whenever I wasn't working, I would head to their
house, some fifty yards from my own, facing the river, to
relax, laugh, and chat idly. It was Wan e' who defined my
kinship ties when he came to my house to invite me to
eat fruits that "my mother" had gathered. I proudly followed him to his house and thereafter began to call him
"'father," his wife "mother," and his children "brother"
and "sister." Immediately all the other Wari' also became
my kin. It was expected that I adopt the classifications of
my siblings—all of those whom my siblings called uncle,
father, mother, nephew, or child, I would call the same. At
that moment, I was not yet aware that Paletó, as a brother
of Wan e', had become my father too. They were not sons
of the same father or the same mother, but Wan e' was
the son of Paletó's mother's sister; for the Wari', this was
a relationship equivalent to brother. Wan e' and Paletó
had grown up living together in several different villages
and were close.

In the brief time we lived together, cut short by his sudden death, Wan e' behaved as a model father, always inviting me to eat whatever food was in his house, and entering and leaving my own, the house of the teacher Edna, without ceremony at any time of day. Very often I awoke in my hammock surrounded by faces, among them that of Wan e', repeating the mantra "coffee, coffee, coffee." I would slowly open my eyes, still sleepy, and, amused, go to make coffee on the single burner stove I had bought in Guajará. After it was brewed, we would all sit around the kitchen's wooden table to talk. One day, a boat arriving from the city brought me a cheese, a treat that I wanted to share with them. After offering them the cheese I heard someone, unaware of my progress in learning the language, ask Wan e' whether I was trying to poison them. By way of reply, I took a piece of cheese and ate it, and Wan e' looked proudly at his apprentice daughter.

At that time, unlike today, the doors of the houses had no locks and people entered and left freely whenever they wanted, so long as one of the house's inhabitants was present. Thefts occurred but were rare. Canoes had owners, but anyone could go to a dock, take a canoe, and set off fishing. What was hunted or fished was immediately distributed to close kin and to the children of other houses, who came to watch the distribution, very often sent by their mothers. I myself, also eager for meat and fish, sent my sons more than once, and I've never forgotten their proud smiles when they returned home with a good portion.

Today, thirty years later, many houses have a television, a diesel generator, and all kinds of objects, ranging from clothes made from synthetic fabrics bought in the city to DVDs and CDs, which need to be locked away when the owner is absent. Some have their own scales, used to weigh pieces of meat, which they sell to neighbors and sometimes even to kin, in exchange for produce from the gardens, but ideally for money. The houses now have windows and a wooden door with a lock, corrugated roofing, and internal divisions made from curtains that create spaces used as bedrooms, furnished with mattresses and beds, rather than mats on the floor as I first remember.

In my first trips, nobody had anything different from anyone else. Manufactured objects were seldom found, sewing machines being a rare exception, used by the women to make colorful chintz dresses. Two or three young men had record players with which they put on lively weekly forró dances, where they would invite me to dance, saying, "Enemy/White woman, dance!" It did not embarrass them to be much shorter than I was. I was delighted to dance with them. They knew how to lead a partner and had great rhythm. It was at the forró dances that I met one of Paletó's daughters, Main Tawi, animated and highly pursued by the young men, dancing barefoot in her short cotton dress. The division by gender at the dances was clear. The girls, dressed the same, were clustered in one corner of the dance floor, waiting to be called by the men, clustered in another corner. The men walked over, took one of the girls by the arm, and they started to dance. As soon as the music ended, they separated immediately, each going back to their corner without looking at the other.

The songs were Brazilian, forró or brega in style, with romantic lyrics or sexual metaphors, which most of the dancers did not understand. I noted this on the day when they took a tape recorder and cassettes on a fishing trip to a lake outside the area. The owner, an Evangelical, of a house near to where we had stopped to fish came to complain directly to me, saying that she did not want those indecent songs played there. That was when I had to translate the lyrics to the Wari', which made them like the songs even more.

Wan e' was physically similar to Paletó. Though a little shorter, he had the same facial shape, with narrow eyes and a broad nose, as well as an open smile. As a shaman, or *pajé*, Wan e' also had another body in the form of a peccary (similar to a wild pig), which walked in the forest and under the rivers while Wan e' slept, or even while he was awake. Let me explain: a peccary to our eyes only, since the animals see themselves as people, with a human body and a social life like that of the Wari'. Wan e' could thus see them as people.

When he perceived that this double life greatly interested me, Wan e' would stop by my house and invite me to accompany him whenever he was summoned to cure someone sick. On arrival, I would stand next to the kin who surrounded the patient, whose head was usually resting in the lap of someone sitting on the stilt palm platform that served as a bed. If the person was seriously ill, his or her kin would lament them through a funeral chant, remembering their feats as though they were already dead. Coming from a world where one seeks to hide the seriousness of the disease from the sick person, always remaining positive about a cure, I was startled by this mode of treatment, especially because it did not exclude small children from the weeping circle.

One day, Maxun Hat, the son of Wan e', was injured during a soccer match. He had broken a rib and was in a lot of pain. After spending some time in the village infirmary, he was carried to the veranda of his house and laid on a plastic mattress brought from the infirmary. His head rested on the lap of his older brother, and his mother lay by his side. Also next to him, seated, was Topa', his wife, who had their six-year-old daughter Juliana in her lap, the same girl who had offered me my first insect larva in the garden. The four shamans from the Negro River manipulated his body, sucking some of its parts and, going outside, spitting out the blood that they, with their special vision, saw accumulated in his back. All of the relatives cried around him, singing the funeral melody, remembering his acts, and lamenting his imminent death. He himself repeated, in the melody of the funeral song, that he was going to die, leaving behind his wife and young daughter. Frightened by the scene, I picked up Juliana and took her outside, wishing to calm her, telling her that her father would be cured, which was indeed what happened.

Some months later, his wife Topa' suffered a miscarriage and was admitted to the Guajará hospital. When I arrived in Guajará, coming from Rio de Janeiro, I went to visit her and offered to send news to her daughter, since I was about to leave for the village. Topa', who was sitting up in bed and talkative, thanked me and asked me to tell Juliana that her mother was going to die. Juliana had become very close to me. She liked necklaces and bracelets, so I called her—as I still do today—*perua*, "female turkey," Rio de Janeiro's slang for someone who wears too much jewelry, associated with the attraction that shiny things supposedly exert on turkeys. At the time, I was unable to pass on her mother's message, not only because it seemed to me that her mother was not seriously ill (in fact, a few days later she was back in the village) but also because I grew up with the idea that children should be spared from suffering whenever possible.

This episode came to mind again almost thirty years later, when in 2015, I was watching a lesson for Wari' students training to be teachers on how to prepare school texts for children. The stories they made up, the White professor taught, could include hardships but should always have a happy ending. Children should not be told stories that ended in tragedy. At that moment, it did not occur to me to ask whether the student teachers agreed. In any event, when the professor asked the class how they should end the stories, the students replied in unison, "and they lived happily ever after."

Like Juliana, other children were always buzzing around me in the Negro-Ocaia River village, and the smaller ones I would carry on my hip, Wari' style. One of them I called "butterfly," *terere*, because she always asked me to draw a butterfly on her arm with my pen. Orowao, a two-year-old, would come to the house every day so I could take her to the river, where we would bathe. Frederico, a small boy, arrived at my house with his shorts torn, asking me to sew them, and Roberto, who today is a city councilor, was always close by, sometimes carrying an enormous boombox on his shoulders. Today I often confuse some of their children, when seeing them for the first time, with their father or mother, losing track of the lapsed time.

In the curing sessions, Wan e' was often accompanied by three shamans from the Negro River: Wao Tokori, also a peccary, Orowam, a jaguar, and Wem Karamain, a trahira fish (also known as a wolf or tiger fish). Whenever possible, the four worked together, inspecting the sick person's body, sucking and spitting out the blood they saw coagulated in some part of the body and removing the fur, food, and decorations of the animals that were trying to carry away the person's double and make them a member of their society. Wan e' made peccary sounds, rubbed his eyes, and with one hand, removed these objects from the sick person's body, transferring them to the other hand, which would remain clenched until he could open his palm outside the house and throw them all away. Sometimes before throwing them out, he or another of the shamans would show people an object, a hair or a seed, that had been extracted from the patient's body. What characterizes the shaman is precisely this visual capacity. Explaining the process of becoming a shaman to me in Portuguese one day, a man defined it as *soltar*—a "freeing" of the eyes—suggesting that the gaze of other people is fixed and limited.

Each of the shamans worked in his own way, in accordance with the behavior of the associated animal. Orowam growled like a jaguar. Wem Karamain, sustained by his arms, lay above the body of the sick person and floated, swimming like a fish. They were not in a trance: the shaman's two bodies could coexist without one of them being taken over by the other. Once in the middle of a cure, I saw Wan e' acting as a peccary. His wife, Orowao Xik Waje, said that she was going home, and Wan e' immediately replied that he would be going soon too, and then returned to his peccary behavior.

At the end of the sessions, the shamans would speak simultaneously about the possible causes of the disease, which, when it affected children, was associated with the breaking of food taboos by the parents, or by the possible sexual partners of the parents, which always caused a commotion and, sometimes, fights between couples. As the wife or husband knew what the other had eaten, since they eat together, the breaking of the taboo, such as eating birds with claws when having a small child, must have occurred outside the conjugal unit, confirming adultery. I would return home with Wan e', sometimes late at night, and I always asked him the next day to tell me the details of what had happened.

In the pauses of our conversations, I would go to the river with his wife to bathe, taking my rose-scented Phebo de Rosas brand soap, which today remains her favorite present. As was typical for most villagers, our movements were closely observed. From time to time, others would ask us, laughing, why we always bathed together. Orowao Xik Waje taught me the correct reply: This is how our bodies are. For the Wari', it is in the body that the tastes, affects, and way of being are located. Bathing together was our way. Many years later, Orowao became my children's grandmother.

41

Orowao Xik Waje, Francisco, and André, 2002

During this period, there was an epidemic of what the Wari' called "strange leaf." People said that young men, trying to seduce the girls, would blow a leaf toward their heads, which made them go mad and act strangely to everyone around them. Worried, the parents took the girls to the shamans to remove the leaves, who then showed the leaves to everyone and exhorted the men not to do the same again. They were placing the young women in danger of being attracted by animals, given their incapacity to recognize real people, an effect of the leaves. Some of these shaman's cures happened during the forró dances, with the record player at high volume, couples dancing, and, in the middle of the dance floor, the sick girl or boy lying on the ground with the shamans around her or him. The final exhortation was also made amid the music and dance, and I was always struck by how this did not perturb the shamans. I understood later that this was the Wari' way of speaking formally. You do not talk directly to the audience, and the audience does not need to give any indication that they are listening. You simply speak, and who wants to hear listens.

I was in my house in Rio de Janeiro, in 1991, when a young man called me from Guajará-Mirim to say that Wan e' had died. The impact and sadness prevented me from asking about the details of his death, and I remember the man trying to console me, saying that Wan e' was now underwater, dancing alongside his dead kin. When I returned to the Negro River in 1992, my closest friends approached me carefully and gave me the news of his death again. I do not remember who told me, upon seeing me cry, that one of the other shamans had already seen Wan e' underwater, that he was rejuvenated, that he had married again and had children. One day he would come to us in his peccary form, offering himself as game to his kin, to then be eaten, revived, and returned to the land of the dead, once more with a young human body. Before they were told about the Christian heaven, this was the cycle of death and life they all shared—leaving and re-turning, always in contact with their kin, whom they sought out to visit even if they could not be recognized by them.

4.
THE HOUSES

Although Paletó entered my life gradually, it felt like I had become deeply connected to him since my very first months at the Negro-Ocaia River village. Our early conversations were almost always mediated by Abrão, who sometimes in his translations struggled to keep up with the enthusiastic engagement of his father. I can clearly remember Paletó's house from those first trips in 1986 and 1987. It was located at the back of the village, far from the river, raised from the ground and constructed, like all the other houses, with stilt palm walls—which were essentially not walls at all, since they let through every sight and sound—and a patawa palm thatch roof. There was no veranda. In front of the house was a wooden stool where, from time to time, I would spot him chatting with other people and his children. I took a photo of him there, smiling, wearing the shirt of a soccer team (the one that my son André was unable to identify). Inside the house was a large, square, cloth mosquito net. It was kept rolled up during the day, revealing the overlapping mats on which Paletó, his wife, his teenage daughters Main Tawi and A'ain Tot, and the children Davi and Ja all slept. Abrão slept apart, in a hammock at the rear of the house. The oldest daughter, Orowao Karaxu, who was married, lived in another house in the same village.

At that time, Paletó also had another house in Ta' Nakot, a site about two hours' walk from the Negro-Ocaia River village, where he lived during the maize planting and harvesting seasons. I went there for the first time in the company of some women to gather honey and inga fruits, and another time to plant maize with Paletó's nephew, A'ain, and his wife, who also had a house in Ta' Nakot. A third house belonged to Awo Kamip, another nephew, who would become pastor of the local church. On these visits, we did not stay to sleep, returning to the village at dusk.

The first time I slept in Ta' Nakot, I had pleaded with Paletó's nephew A'ain to take me with them. In those early days, the Wari' were skeptical of my ability to live outside the village. A little put out, I think, A'ain, a tall, slender man with a very broad face, abruptly arrived at my house early one morning, barefoot, wearing just his shorts and clutching a bow and some arrows in his hand. He said simply: "Let's go!" Taken by surprise, I hurriedly packed a rucksack with my sleeping bag, mosquito net, and some spare clothes. At the start of the trek, I ran behind him and the others who accompanied us. A'ain soon dropped back behind me, though, respecting my pace and protecting me. At some point, when I saw him leave the trail and enter the forest, announcing, "I'm going to shit," I stopped to wait for him, allowing the others to walk out of sight ahead, apprehensive, afraid that he would vanish, but he reemerged from the dense foliage and we continued on. Upon arriving, I was lodged in an open-walled house, still under construction, and there I spent some of the best days of my life, naively thinking that their talk of nocturnal jaguar attacks was just their playful way of trying to scare me.

There I helped them plant and they offered me maize to make my first maize cake. Mimicking the women, I sat with my legs crossed in front of a thick wooden board, which served as a surface for rolling from one side to the other the oval stone used to grind the kernels placed on top of the wood with a little water. A small pot off to the side served as a receptacle for the ground paste, freeing up the wood for more kernels. Afterwards, the paste was tipped into an elongated container made from palm leaves, sewed together with thorns, and wrapped tight with strands from the leaves. This container could then be cooked in a pan of water, or roasted on a grill over an open fire. I preferred the latter, but both maize cakes are delicious. The same paste, when cooked directly in a pan and mixed with more water, turned into a sweet maize drink (*chicha*). If macerated by hand and masticated, then left to rest for a few days, the mash became *chicha azeda*, a sour maize drink, fermented and alcoholic. That first time, I ground the maize successfully but was unable to sew the leaf containers, which made the women laugh. But they soon came to my assistance. On returning to the village after a few days, the news quickly spread that I had made maize cake, and people once again went about exclaiming that I had finally turned Wari'. They were even more thrilled when Beto came to visit me at the start of 1987 and I prepared maize cake for him. Now I was definitely a Wari' woman, they said, making maize cake for my husband.

My lack of skill in manual tasks was always abundantly apparent and even now, after decades living among them, I cannot make a maize cake container that does not leak. Wari' women, by contrast, are extremely resourceful. When we went to gather honey, they would quickly fashion an impermeable container from the leaves of a particular type of banana tree, and also make a strap from vines for each of us to transport our honey home. Traveling to Paletó's house in Ta' Nakot one time, accompanied only by my younger sister, Ja, a storm caught us mid-journey. Ja, then six years old, asked for my penknife and cut multiple wild banana leaves with long stems. These she stuck in the ground to construct a temporary shelter, which indeed shielded us from the downpour. I shall never forget the contrast between her slender appearance, hair cut short and bangs cropped in the style of Wari' women, and her decisive manner and strong voice, which characterize her to this day. I arrived in Ta' Nakot with my sleeping bag almost dry, although my clothes were less fortunate.

I vividly remember the various times that I walked the trail to Ta' Nakot, the easy laughter in my conversations with Abrão and other young people, which transported me back to my own teenage years and friends, and made me feel completely at home. One time when we were on the path, they asked me to teach them the anthem of the Flamengo soccer club. After singing the anthem, I taught them some short Brazilian popular songs that came to mind. We sang the entire journey, repeating the songs numerous times so that they could memorize the lyrics.

During this period, I moved houses in the village more than once. Edna, the teacher who took me in when I first arrived, married, and moved to the house of Valdir, the Funai representative at the Rio Negro-Ocaia Post. Other teachers soon arrived and occupied the two bedrooms of Edna's house. As no family invited me to live in their house, perhaps thinking I would not accept such an invitation during these early months when I still did not know them well, Valdir offered me a space in the toolshed, which I spent several days cleaning to render it habitable. Unlike Edna's house, the shed had no running water or bathroom (which, in her house, was outside, close to the back door). I ended up carrying buckets and buckets of water up from the river to cook and drink. Like the other women and children, I would go to the river around midday with a bowl filled with lunch plates and a bucketful of dirty laundry. We would stay there talking and bathing for more than two hours, carefree chatter that taught me many things about Wari' life. The lack of a bathroom for day-to-day use was a little more complicated. My neighbors and I had used a thicket located close to the house of a family from another ethnic group, the OroWin, who, after a massacre in the 1970s, had been brought to live at the Rio Negro-Ocaia Post. Although the family used the same area of vegetation, large and comfortable, one day, after an argument between myself and the man of the house, he angrily cleared the bushes, forcing me and the others, as well as themselves, to walk quite far to the next thicket every time we needed to relieve ourselves.

Sometimes the other sections of the shed, separated from mine by half-walls, were occupied by visitors, especially manual workers who spent days in the village doing work on the Funai houses. I would then move to the house of one Wari' friend or other—now not just invited but obliged by them, who would come to fetch me, worried about my safety. I stayed in the houses of Xatoji, Topa', Maxun Hat, and Juliana, and remember our conversations at night as we lay covered by our mosquito nets. Early in the morning, the macaw parrots that they bred would wake us up, imitating the sounds of peccaries. I don't know why I never stayed in Paletó's house at the post—perhaps because back then, as I was closer to Wan e' and his family, I stayed in his son's house.

On other trips, I found the teachers' house available again and, by luck, one such occasion happened to be the first time I took my son Francisco, then a year and a half old, in 1992. I slept on the ground with my mosquito net, while he slept in a collapsible canvas cot with a built-in mosquito net. The next year, the house newly occupied, Francisco, Beto, and I lodged in the radio cabin, a small room adjacent to the head of post's house.

In the late 1990s, after more than thirty years of living in houses at the post, Paletó and his family decided to found a new village, downstream, close to the mouth of the Negro River, at a place called Boca, on the edge of the Indigenous territory.* They told me that they moved because of the chicken thefts that began to occur at the post and that prevented them from breeding their own flock. Orowao Karaxu and her family were already living some distance away, on the shores of the Mamoré, where her husband, Orowao Kun, was working for Funai.

---

* Most Indigenous peoples in Brazil live in demarcated and protected lands recognized by the government as the territory traditionally occupied by their ethnic group.

Francisco and an anteater pup, 1992

I first visited the Boca settlement in July 2001, on a brief stay of less than a month, mainly just wanting to see them after five years away. The pilot Chagas once again transported me there and, along with my brothers, helped unload my things and set up my sleeping mat (which, now that I was older, I had started to use), sleeping bag, and mosquito net in Paletó's house, on a section of the stilt palm platform. Many people lived in the house, including Abrão's parents-in-law, who would later build a house for themselves nearby. There were two pregnant women in the house: Abrão's wife, Tem Xao, and our sister Ja. I recall this clearly because the three of us frequently found ourselves together outside the house at midnight, crouched down to pee.

Years earlier, I had played an important role in Abrão's marriage. Everything began when it seemed (so the others remarked) that he liked a girl from the Negro River. A marriage had been arranged, however, for him with another young woman: his younger sister Main Tawi's husband's sister. Although marriage did not involve a wedding ceremony as such, in those days the kin of both spouses would meet and, standing in a circle around the bride and groom, who both sat in the middle, would address the couple—saying, for example, that the bride should make food for her husband and look after him, while he should hunt, fish, and always provide her with food. With everyone gathered, Abrão vanished, hiding in a cousin's house. So they asked me, his older sister, to try to convince him to attend. They managed to bring Abrão to my house, which at that time was the toolshed. We closed the door and I made a speech in the style of Wari' kin. I said that he was now an adult man, that it was time for him to marry, and that he could not leave the girl waiting there with all the kin around her. Abrão repeated that he did not want to marry, arguing that he had plans to study and travel. Finally, he relented, and we headed off together to the site of the gathering. Standing next to him, I noticed that Abrão did not move when his bride's kin told him to take her home. So I whispered in his ear, in Wari': "Call her!" He went over to her, took her gently by the arm, and led her home. Today I doubt I would be willing to play the role that I did that day, but, luckily for me, Abrão seems to have liked the outcome. He named his first daughter Aparecida.

On that brief visit to Paletó's house in 2001, I decided not to work, but instead to spend the days pleasurably, idly passing time. I would awaken, fold my mosquito net and tie it up high, roll up my sleeping bag and mat, and walk down the bank with a little agate mug to the stream I used to brush my teeth and make my tea. Midday, I would go down to the stream again to bathe with the girls and at night I reassembled my sleeping gear. I became so lazily contented that I stopped combing my hair and remained that way for some days. In my mind, I was becoming a spirit of nature, mirrorless and happy, until Paletó, with great tact, sat down beside me to say that I was a pretty woman, and that I should comb my hair because it was becoming unsightly.

Thirteen years later, on the last visit I made to the Negro River in July 2014, Paletó was still living at Boca, but now in the house of Ja, his youngest daughter, along with his wife, To'o, and their son Davi. About one hundred yards away, a distance walked each day by Paletó with the help of a walking stick, were the houses of Abrão and Main Tawi. It had been six years since I last visited the Negro River, though I had met Paletó in 2012, in Rio de Janeiro, already somewhat debilitated but still very lucid and talkative. When I climbed up the riverbank toward Ja's house, announcing as usual, "Dad, I've arrived," I noticed that he was facing away, squatting in front of the house, without turning toward me as I approached. Alarmed, I asked Ja whether he recognized me—whether he still remembered people, whether he had a "heart," or thought, in the Wari' language. Ja laughed and said yes, obviously. He would turn around to talk to me soon enough. She then placed two stools, one in front of the other, and asked me to sit down, facing Paletó. Paletó sat, held my shoulder, and began to cry in a spoken lament that reminded me of the funeral chant, saying that his body was no use for anything anymore, and how sad he was that I had to see him in such a condition. It was the first time I had seen the effects of the disease on his body. His gaze was somewhat vacant, his walk difficult, his joints rigid.

The house was raised from the ground, with a large veranda on which a gas stove was placed, and was internally
divided into two bedrooms opening onto the veranda, each
with a double bed, a mattress, and a mosquito net. On one of
them slept Ja, her husband, a young man of the Aruá ethnic
group, Ja's older daughter, a teenager, whom she'd had while
still single, the couple's two younger daughters, and Davi,
Ja's brother; on the other, Paletó and To'o. Both Davi and
the girls may have circulated between the two beds and the
house's two bedrooms without a fixed berth, a commonplace
situation among the Wari'.

I always liked Davi a lot. He was seven when I first met
him, a sensitive boy who paid attention to everything and
loved to draw. Davi had suffered from infantile paralysis as a
baby and never walked. While he was still small, his parents
carried him on their backs to the gardens or the river, but as

he grew it became difficult to carry him about. They tried a wheelchair, but it proved useless on the uneven ground of the village paths. It ended up a children's toy, repurposed as a way to race downhill. Davi became a strong man, always good humored despite the enormous limitations in his life. While once there had been people to carry him to a canoe to accompany the others on fishing trips, when he could display his skills as a rower and a fisherman, today there was no one able to carry him, not even to bathe in the river, leaving him dependent on help for every activity. The last time I saw him, in 2014, he had bleached his hair and with his disability pension had bought a satellite antenna and television, on which we watched the World Cup soccer matches, one of the rare moments in my life when I enthusiastically watched a soccer game. During one of the World Cup matches, I decided to make a cake filled with guava paste to be baked in the oven of their house. When I distributed pieces to everyone, amid our yells of support for Brazil, Ja, always close to her brother, made sure that Davi received his share. I know how much Paletó and To'o worried about Davi—about who to leave him with when they visited other villages, or about his food and bathing. Eventually, Ja assumed the care of Davi.

Paletó and To'o's room in Ja's house was almost entirely occupied by the bed, with a small shelf at the back where they stored various objects. Most of their clothes were kept in a suitcase under the bed, where To'o also carefully placed the items that I had brought on the trip as presents for Paletó. Among them was a red scarf given by my biological father, which Paletó adored and decided to use immediately, even in the strong heat of that July. Now and then, Paletó would lie down to sleep, and ask me to bring him some water, which he drank with a straw.

On the side wall of Paletó's room, someone had hung two framed photos. One of them showed Ja and her husband; the other, one of her small daughters, her brother Davi, and a niece, Main's daughter. These intrigued me not only because it was a novelty for the Wari' to have photos of themselves on display but also because they were dressed in formal Western clothing. Ja was wearing a full-length bridal gown, while her husband wore a suit and tie. In the other photo, Davi appeared dressed in a suit, standing up straight, as though his legs were not atrophied. The girls were wearing Western party costumes with billowing lacy skirts. I asked Ja whether they had bought these costumes and was surprised to learn that it was a photomontage, the specialty of a photographer in Guajará-Mirim popular among the Wari'.

I recently learned that those kinds of photomontage are popular not only among the Wari': in the house of a friend from Rio de Janeiro, the mother of a boy who is unable to walk, I saw a large photo of her child standing up with adolescent's clothes and shoes, a present from his nanny. At that moment I realized something, probably obvious to most but that had not occurred to me before: photos are not necessarily faithful reproductions of reality. They can project parallel, desired and imagined realities. The art of photography was appropriated by the Wari' not because of photography's power to capture images, to act as a mirror to the world, but due to its capacity to transform, to project bodies into another world, an idea evocative of the shamans and their alternative bodies. Indeed, the Wari' term for any reflection or image is the same term used for a person's double, which lives in another world, and the double can have different characteristics from the person, such as being able to walk when the person cannot, for example, as with my friend's son. One shaman of great repute, Maxun Kworain, had atrophied legs and frequently seemed exhausted, attributed to the fact that his peccary double, with perfectly healthy legs, had been running around in the forest. When, in Rio, Paletó and I visited Sugarloaf Mountain, Paletó was surprised by a portraitist, who without pausing to ask for permission, took a photo of him and Abrão. Seeing what the man was selling there, Paletó remarked: "Someone made our images, took our doubles to put on a plate."

On that same visit to Boca village in 2014, I discovered that many people displayed photos in their houses of the kind I had seen in Ja's house. I was amazed to see one of a recently deceased old man, dressed in a suit amid a Swiss-type

landscape with mountains and a waterfall. Next to this carefully framed picture was another photo of his wife, also deceased, in the same landscape, wearing a long dress. I recall
that in 1986 the older Wari' frequently would not let me
take photos of them, saying that when they died, the sight
of these photos would sadden their children. I was left trying to understand what had changed so radically over these
thirty years for the Wari' now to display photos of the dead
in their houses. Probably, as in the above cases, these images
project a desired reality: in the case of the dead, an afterlife
in the Christian heaven, a paradisiacal place associated with
the world of the Whites, where everyone wears beautiful
clothes and shoes.

The house in Boca was not the last in which Paletó
lived. He spent his final year living with his oldest daughter,
Orowao Karaxu. Having moved from the Mamoré River, she
was then living at Linha 26, one of the villages accessed by
small roads branching out from the BR 364 highway, which
connects Porto Velho to Guajará-Mirim, and where one can
still glimpse the tracks of the famous Madeira-Mamoré Railway poking up through the asphalt. Although I call her my
older sister, Orowao is probably close to my age, born a little
before contact with the Whites. When I first met her on the
Negro River in 1986, she was already the mother of four
girls and, soon after, three boys. For a long time, these were
Paletó's only grandchildren. Orowao's oldest daughter, Toko
Pi'am, an incredibly beautiful girl, was one of my first friends,
but died around age fifteen, already the mother of a daughter, due to a second pregnancy which proved to be ectopic.
Orowao's third daughter, Tokohwet, was my companion at
home during many nights, sent by her mother so I would

not have to sleep alone. I lost Tokohwet's company when she became ill with malaria, an epidemic in the Negro-Ocala River village at the time, and was forced to spend many days lying in a hammock with a high fever and vomiting.

I have no idea how I avoided catching malaria, given how many sick people there were around me during my first trips to the village in 1986 and 1987. I can only attribute this to the mosquito repellent that I always carried about in a small bag with my notebook and a pen, and also to the long trousers, sleeved shirts, sneakers, and socks that I put on every day at dusk when the mosquitos went into their feeding frenzy, sometimes even biting through my shirt. And undoubtedly to the mosquito net. This precious, finely woven mesh was not only useful against mosquitos—it also offered protection from cockroach invasions.

One such invasion occurred in 1987, on, of all days, my birthday in April. At the time I was living in the toolshed. I slept on a mat on the floor, lined with a sleeping bag. When I opened my eyes, the mosquito net, a light-yellow color, was dark, as though day had not yet arrived. It took me a while to realize that it was thick with cockroaches. Once I'd gotten over the initial shock, I lay there wondering how to make my escape. Finally the unrelenting need to pee forced me to jump up, fling open the mosquito net, and furiously brush away the cockroaches that fell on my head. That experience toughened me—I became so at ease with the insects that I could kill them with my bare hands rather than whacking them with a sandal.

I never lived in Orowao's house in Linha 26, but I did visit her in January 2005, when I spent a stretch of time nearby, in Linha 29, in the house where Paletó lived with his family for around two years. They had been drawn to the region's abundant natural resources, and also were acting in response to Funai's encouragement to occupy threatened areas of Indigenous territory, the natural features and policy incentives that had led Orowao and her family to that region, far from where she was born.

This small village had only two houses: one inhabited by Paletó, To'o, and Davi, and the other by their daughter A'ain Tot, her husband, and the couple's children. Also living there was our younger sister Ja, then still single, and her daughter Leila, and at the time of my visit, two nephews were also spending time there. I stayed in A'ain Tot's house with my sons, André, six years old, and Francisco, fourteen. The house had been constructed in the old style with a stilt palm floor and walls, a straw roof, and no internal divisions. Generously, they let us use one side of the house. At night, the straw mats on their side of the house seemed to be covered end to end with people, draped by a single, large, square mosquito net. The scene in the morning, when, one by one, they emerged from the mosquito net, reminded me of a beguiling moment from one of my favorite films, *Nanook of the North*, in which an endless stream of people, along with one or two dogs, emerge from a single canoe. In our corner of the house, I hung a hammock for each of the boys and, in the middle of them, on the ground, placed my mattress, covered by my attached funnel-shaped mosquito net. The boys' hammocks already contained their own mosquito nets. In the cramped space, when the boys moved at night, my net, hung up in the middle, would sway with their movements and wake me up.

This did not bother me. On the contrary, I relished the feeling of all of us being together. Up until a few years ago, when my back started to give me problems, I could feel at home anywhere. It was enough just to have a corner to spread out my things, which I would arrange in such a way I could find them by touch even in the dark: canteen, torch, insect repellent, soap, and my bag with the notebook and recorder. The only thing that bothered me in the house was a battery-powered radio. Every day it switched on around five in the morning, tuned to an Evangelical radio station. The radio signal was weak, so the volume was turned up to maximum, and the announcer alternated between whispers and yells, which invariably made me leap out of bed. As a guest, I was reluctant to ask them to turn the radio down, but today, older and less tolerant, I am certain I would.

Years earlier I had lived through a tense moment with A'ain Tot, who was by nature quiet and shy. During a voyage we made together to the Lage Novo village, this young woman, who rarely said a thing, decided to tell her parents that she was pregnant and did not know who the father was. Paletó was furious with her; feeling sorry for her, I was driven to intervene, asking for him to be calm. After all, she was already pregnant and now frightened too. Tempers eventually subsided. The baby was born and was raised by the mother and grandparents until A'ain Tot married Moroxin, who adopted the daughter as his own. During those days when we shared the house, Moroxin, a good hunter, would sometimes leave with his rifle in the morning and return in the afternoon with killed game. One time, he arrived with a porcupine which, even after death, hurled quills at André when he approached curiously. Extracting them from his skin amid his desperate crying was something of an ordeal. To console him, Paletó told how

Francisco, his book, and a monkey tooth necklace, 2005

in the past a woman, unable to see well at night, mistook
a porcupine for an armadillo and sat on it to capture it.
The quills penetrated her anus and vagina, and her screams
were terrible to hear.

It was a period of learning for both of my boys. Francisco was already well accustomed to the food and had a
predilection for agouti, a small rodent. Now a teenager, he
alternated between reading one of the many books he had
brought with him, lying around the house, and taking long
baths in the stream, where he became a child again, rolling
down the bank into the water. One day he told me that he
liked it there more than Cambridge, in England, where we
had lived the previous year. André, then six years old, used
to take his small bow and arrows, given to him by Paletó,
and head into the nearby forest, saying that he would catch
food for us that day. He had no luck. But his grandfather

Paletó was filled with pride nonetheless, just as he was on observing Francisco's growing skill with the bow, the result of his teaching since he was little. Many years earlier, I had filmed Francisco, then three years old, clutching a small bow and arrow, with Paletó holding his arms behind for him to aim at something. Lots of children milled around and would run off each time Francisco pointed the bow somewhere, afraid of the arrow. One of those children was Jânio, Main Tawi's oldest son and Paletó's cherished grandson, exactly the same age as Francisco. I have a photo of the two of them aged a year and a half, sitting in front of a plate of fish. Jânio ate tiny portions, taking care not to swallow the fishbones. Francisco, not knowing how to eat, needed my help to extract the bones.

Paletó and André, 2002

It was at Linha 29 that André ate insect larvae for the first time, roasted and rolled in leaves. Everyone waited to see if he liked them, observing him while he chewed. He disappointed them—he did not. His favorite delicacy continued to be the little hands of roasted monkeys, which he would savor for hours, eating slowly, plucking the meat from between the fingers, as the boys had taught him. He also learned about the importance of food when there is no supermarket nearby, no packed larder. One time, the men brought a macaw parrot back from a hunt, which, though injured, was still alive. Killing it would require plenty of skill, since it could still fly away from its captors. Paletó decided that Francisco would be the one to kill it, so he could learn. Wielding an adult bow, Francisco struck the macaw when it landed on the ground. Perhaps because he liked the macaw, or considered it a pet, André began to cry on witnessing its torment, and I decided to take him away to bathe in the stream while they finished the job. Later, To'o invited us to eat. André was told that the aluminum pan in front of us contained not only the macaw but also the infant monkey we had been feeding with powdered milk for days. To my surprise, he did not refuse to eat, and even insisted that we place on his plate a portion of macaw and a portion of monkey.

Our days passed slowly with baths in the stream, short walks in the forest, and keeping an eye out for rain in case we needed to hastily remove our things from the clothesline. Paletó was very busy, harvesting Brazil nuts all morning and returning home in the afternoon. Whenever he stayed home, I would rush over to his house with my recorder to hear his stories. I was interested in systematically recording versions of all the myths he knew. And there were a lot. Our deliberate pace was interrupted by an outbreak of diarrhea that affected me and the boys, probably due to eating some food brought from the city that apparently had spoiled. Fortunately, the Wari' had not shared it.

Everyone looked after us. Paletó went to the forest to gather the bark of a vine for his wife to make a reddish astringent tea, which quickly cured me and Francisco but not André. Already Christians, they always included us in the prayers they said before meals, especially for André, who was still feeling unwell. Although his state did not appear worrying to me, I decided to return to the city when I found him sitting on a trunk, some distance from the house, with his little hands clasped together, asking God, Wari' style, to cure his diarrhea. He was no longer finding the adventure much fun.

Davi, who controlled the Funai radio, which was located in the house of his parents, was able to ask for a car to be sent to fetch us. These long-distance communication radios intrigued me. They are the only means of communication in most Wari' villages, at least in all those where I have lived. They provide news of sick relatives, tell who is traveling where, announce the day that the boat is leaving with supplies. One day, in February 2008, after hearing one woman tell another, by radio, that she was missing her, I wrote in my field notebook, probably still inspired by the book I had just finished reading, *Atonement*, by Ian McEwan:

The telephone of the forest. Such a precarious form of communication, so limited. You have to say just the essential, and very clearly, because it is difficult to hear. So beautiful this minimalist conversation, that contains so many unspoken thoughts.

That time at Linha 29 the radio was as efficient as ever and the Funai car arrived the same day. As it was no more than two hours' drive to the city from there, I took only a canteen of water for the journey, and left all the food with the Wari'. On the way, the driver entered a village to pick up someone else, and there the car broke down. To my surprise, he had no toolbox with him, and the tiny village had no radio. Moreover, it was completely empty. Stuck there, with André weak and with little water, I felt a surge of heroic maternity and decided to grab a bicycle I had seen thrown on the ground and take to the road in search of help, not without first asking Francisco to take care of his brother and giving him the canteen. The expedition might have taken hours, as the nearest houses were some distance away, but luckily, not much later, I met a man on a motorbike, and asked him to help us with his tools. In less than an hour we were back on the road again, and I learned never to take any trip without water or food—a compulsive habit that I maintain to this day, even in the city, to the astonishment of my friends.

In all of these houses, as well as in the different houses in which I have lived in Rio de Janeiro, Paletó told me, at various times and in various ways, his life history. So I shall begin to tell it here, choosing among narratives recorded on tape cassettes, MiniDiscs, and, more recently, digital recorders.

5.
ESCAPING DEATH FOR
THE FIRST TIME

IT WAS THE EARLY 1930S. The world was tense and fragmented. Recession in the United States, totalitarian regimes emerging in Europe, and a war being gestated. In Brazil, Getúlio Vargas, who would quickly become sympathetic to those totalitarian regimes, came to power with the 1930 revolution. Rondônia, where our history unfolds, was not yet a state. It was the setting, though, for numerous political disputes for control of the border region and for clashes between the Indigenous populations and rubber tappers. The latter had arrived from the northeast of the country during the First World War in search of the rubber that supplied various industrial sectors, the war industry among them. Guajará-Mirim, previously a settlement called Esperidião Marques, had been officially declared a town in 1929. The Wari' lands, already bisected by the construction of the Madeira-Mamoré Railway in the first years of the twentieth century, were being continually invaded by rubber tappers, and, like their neighbors, some of the Wari' had either been killed or been captured and taken to be displayed in the town. A short while before Paletó was born, a Wari' man called Maxun Taparape, then still a child, had seen his brother killed by the Whites and was himself abducted during the same attack, taken to live in rubber-tapper camps and in the urban area. When he eventually returned, he was unable to recognize people or even the language anymore, and it was with me that Paletó saw him for the first time after this abduction. The same happened to other children.

Unaware of the fraught global and national situations but suffering the consequences of their repercussions in the Amazon rainforest, Paletó's parents' group had abandoned their original lands nearer to the Pacaás Novos River where the presence of invaders was increasingly difficult to avoid. They moved farther from the river to live along smaller streams. At the moment of his birth, Paletó's parents were in the middle of a trek through forest with other families, heading toward a place called Mapat, where they had planted maize. A boy sent to scout ahead had come back to report that the maize had already grown and was now sprouting. They decided it was time to move there and build some new houses, where they would live until all the maize was consumed.

They were moving, which meant that they were traveling with everything they had: baskets with old maize, bows, arrows, files, ceramic pots, and stone axes. I assume that they didn't carry sleeping mats—these could be made rapidly on arrival. As they did not wear any type of clothing, save for a vine sometimes wrapped around a man's waist to tie up his foreskin, they carried no fabrics, although they did have a spindle to spin cotton, used to make adornments for their bows and to wrap around their arms during festivals. Undoubtedly, they carried a length of wood with a glowing ember, or burning resin wrapped in leaves, since they did not know how to produce fire. If the fire went out, they would have to fetch some from another locality. This was always a risk until after contact and their discovery of matches, later followed by lighters, always highly desired.

Women bore the heaviest weight, since they were the ones who carried small children on their waist, held close by a vine draped over the opposite shoulder. They also carried the cargo basket, supported on their back and fastened around their forehead by a strap. This basket was generally filled with maize or wild fruits when used on gathering expeditions. On the longer treks, as in the case of Paletó's family, the baskets might contain all their belongings, such as ceramic pots, an oval stone to grind maize, some stone axes, and even bird feathers for adornments, mixed among the maize cobs. Paletó's mother, with her swollen belly, was probably weighed down in this way, as I saw happen with various pregnant women on my travels with them through the forest. Men sometimes carried a basket on their back, the strap wrapped around their chest rather than their forehead. Generally they did so when transporting roasted game meat after lengthier expeditions and, in the past, enemy flesh, taken home to be eaten by those who had not taken part in the war expedition. Very often this basket was improvised in the forest from leaves and vines. In the case of this journey, the women were probably carrying the children in slings and all the belongings in their baskets, as well as the fire in one of their hands. This left the men free with their bows and arrows, ready to rush after any prey that might appear.

As night fell, the couple and those accompanying them stopped to sleep next to a stream, lying on palm leaves arranged on the ground next to the fire. This was when Paletó's mother, Orowao Karaxu, a name later passed on to his own eldest daughter, entered labor with Paletó. He was not her first child. The eldest, Manim, had been born when Orowao, his mother, was still very young, "like you when you had Francisco," Paletó added helpfully. Manim was followed by a girl and, after Paletó, another girl, who would become mother to Awo Kamip, today the main Evangelical pastor of the Rio Negro-Ocaia Post.

Paletó's mother was from the OroNao' territorial group. O'Werek, his father, had migrated while still young from a neighboring territory occupied by the OroAt group to live among his mother's kin. This was the region in which they were walking at the time of Paletó's birth. I should explain that the Wari' are divided into eight groups, which were related to specific neighboring territories in the past. These are the OroNao', OroEo, OroAt, OroWaram, OroWaramXijein, OroMon, OroJowin, and OroKao'OroWaji. At that time, marriages between people from different territorial groups, though they occurred, were less frequent. So although they knew each other well, spoke the same language, and took part in festivals together, they differed in terms of their accents, the versions of the myths they told, how they built their houses, and in their food taboos.

Everyone recalls that Paletó's father lived for so long among his mother's kin that his OroAt accent was no longer noticeable. People went as far as to say that he had turned OroNao'. This was clearly shown by the choice of the group to which his children belong; unlike what usually happens with children from mixed marriages, who join the father's group, Paletó, along with his brothers and sisters, were Oro-Nao', like their mother. In the 1990s, when ID cards were issued to them, a missionary responsible for listing their names mistakenly applied the rule that children belong to their father's group. Much to his astonishment, Paletó became Watakao' OroAt. Likewise, his children had the name OroAt associated with their names, apart from Abrão, who flatly refused to accept this fate. Having lived all his life as OroNao', Paletó used to playfully imitate the accent of his OroAt kin, who were also distinguished by building their houses very high, accessed by a ladder.

At dawn on the day of his birth, his father O'Werek left to hunt birds, as is customary among Wari' men when their wives enter labor, which they should not witness. Moreover, the broth from the cooked birds can be given to the mother to eat after the birth. Leaving to hunt is the definitive gesture of assuming paternity. Men who do not wish to assume fatherhood, alleging that another man sired the baby, simply remain close to the house during the birth. Staying there, among other people, were O'Werek's younger brother Torein, as well as a young woman, To'o Min, who helped the woman giving birth, her aunt, whom she called mother.

After cutting the umbilical cord with a bamboo blade, they noted that the baby had a large lump on the side of his forehead. Seeing the boy, his uncle Torein got ready to shoot him with an arrow, pulling the cord of his bow in his direction. To'o Min, the girl, with the baby in her hands, not yet washed, ran into the forest, trying to save the newborn. Torein followed her but was unable to catch up. In the camp where the birth had taken place was Toro, whom Paletó would also come to call father. Toro was a capuchin monkey shaman—that is, he had a double with a capuchin monkey body, living among the animals. As soon as To'o Min, having eluded Torein, returned with the newborn, Toro asked her to wash him, looked at him and said: "Our son's head is just swollen, it's nothing! I'm going to cut [the lump] off!" So he took a bamboo blade and sliced it, removing its content with his hands, which looked to him like coagulated blood. Paletó told me he had cried when the lump was sliced off, but then laughed at what he'd said because he certainly did not remember what he felt in his first hours of life.

Toro handed the baby to the mother and only then was he placed on her breast to feed, an important recognition of the child's humanity. Disabled and orphaned children were killed even before they were first breastfed, since there would be nobody to feed or carry them. I witnessed the huge difficulties caused by, and suffered among, teenagers and adults without motor autonomy, including Paletó's own son, Davi. This is even true in the more recent era when large distances between one dwelling and another are no longer traversed by treks in the forest, but by canoes, either rowed or powered by *rabetas*, small outboard motors. If Paletó had been killed before he was breastfed, his funeral would have been different from those of properly Wari' children and adults. He would not have been wept over and delicately eaten by his in-laws or distant kin with chopsticks. Instead, he could be eaten by his own kin, like Torein, for example, except for his mother. In my house in Rio de Janeiro, during one of our didactic enactments of funerary cannibalism, the deceased was precisely a fatherless baby, who was strangled to death by the maternal uncle, as instructed by the grandfather. After being washed with sand to remove every trace of blood, the infant was roasted on a grill, still fresh, as the Wari' say to refer to a body that has not rotted, and eaten by the grandfather himself, who now and again would crouch down to cry, assuming the position of a grieving grandfather. The mother—a role that I assumed in our theatre—cried squatting down, far from the scene, but did nothing to oppose her father's decision.

In the afternoon of the day he was born, his father, O'Werek, arrived carrying some small birds. To'o Min, who called him older brother, although she was his distant kin, ran toward him to say that Torein had wanted to shoot "our son," that she had fled with him, and that Toro had finally cut off the lump. O'Werek angrily went to Torein and asked him why he had done that. He replied: "I thought it was a strange child, a ghost." The next day, Torein went to see the baby and was filled with remorse: "Why did I want to shoot my older brother's son? I was crazy." As he called himself a believer (an Evangelical) at the moment of this narrative, Paletó added: "It was as happened at the birth of Jesus, with the ancient Whites." It was then that the father held him in his arms, another important signal of acceptance of paternity.

At this point he still had no name. Some days later, he was called Pixon, which had been the name of a dead relative. Undoubtedly someone who died long ago—the names of the recent dead were never spoken so as not to cause their kin pain. Over the course of his life, Paletó changed his name multiple times, either because someone with the same name had died, or because there was a suspicion of sorcery, which is premised on the sorcerer's knowledge of the victim's name. After Pixon, he had the following names: Tem Xini, Wao Hwara Winain, Pariri, Mijain Wam, Wan Hon OroNao', Manim (probably after the death of his brother with this name), Wao Wi, Tokorom Xok, and Watakao' Oromixik. When, after hearing the list, I asked him why he had so many names, he gave one of the most common Wari' responses to this kind of question: "It's our way."

When I was compiling a genealogy of the Wari' of the Negro River, this practice of changing names seriously hindered my work, since some people would refer to a particular person by his or her childhood name, and others would cite later names. I therefore spent weeks thinking that some people had been sired by different fathers, when in fact it was the same father with different names. Living with them day to day, I perceived that the name change was assimilated slowly. When Pakao', Paletó's brother's wife, died, a coresident with the same name began to call herself Moroxin We. It took a while for me to get her name right when I addressed her. Similarly, I noted that my Wari' friends would also refer to her as Pakao' from time to time, though never in front of the widower: he would be distraught to hear this name pronounced. With the passing of time and the gradual healing of the pain, Pakao's daughter changed her name and took on her mother's.

This changing of names was such a commonplace event that in 2003, during an expedition to the region of the Laje River, one man told me that when they heard thunder, everyone changed their names. Although close kin who have already died remain the ideal namers, today Wari' names also originate from older people who are still alive, passed to their grandchildren. It was during the aforementioned Laje River expedition that Paletó gave me one of the names of his mother, Moroxin Xererem, to substitute for the name that had been given to me by my late father Wan e' many years earlier, To'o Orowak, the same name as his daughter. But my new name did not catch on: that is, nobody called me by the name after that day, and, as far as I know, the new names adopted there at the Laje River by my friends met the same fate.

Today, along with the Wari' name, many children also receive a Brazilian name, initially a demand of the Whites who interacted with them and found it difficult to comprehend the Indigenous names when they needed to write them on their forms and record cards. The Wari' have turned this imposition in their favor, successfully expanding their stock of names and always assuring a supply of original names for their children, protecting them from sorcery attacks targeted at others, since an infant's life may be threatened if they mistakenly reply to the call of a sorcerer addressing their namesake.

In the past, as soon as the baby received a name, the mother also changed hers since she would begin to be called by the composite "with + name of the baby," a name that she would keep until the birth of her next child. The name Orowao Karaxu, by which Paletó referred to his mother, was probably her childhood name. At the time of Paletó's birth, his mother was called "*kam* Tokohwet," meaning "with Tokohwet," the name of the daughter who preceded Paletó. Following his birth, she became "*kon* Pixon," "with Pixon," Paletó's first name. Watakao' was his last Wari' name, before adopting the name of the only clothing that enchanted him, the *paletó*, the jacket.

Orowao Karaxu remained for some days lying on the same spot where the birth had been, always on fresh leaves. The Wari' take great care to ensure that people who bleed or who deal with blood do not enter the forest, since its distinctive aroma can be smelled from afar by jaguars, who then make the person their prey. Although Paletó did not mention these details, this may be why they had moved as quickly as possible to the new dwelling in Mapat. In the past, the food taboos respected by a woman who had recently given birth were extremely strict. She did not eat game meat or various types of fish. The father, respecting the same interdictions, had to avoid expending too much effort or traveling far, since the baby's double could follow him and become lost in the forest. Neither did he lie next to his wife, so as to protect himself from the blood. Today, mothers who have just given birth spend the first few days inside the cloth mosquito net under which they had their baby. I also presume that there are no more food prohibitions since all of these were suspended in Christian life.

The lump on the head was not Paletó's only health problem. As he told me, as a small boy he suffered from something that the Wari' call a lack of sense, or madness, which they associate with a defect in the person's sight. This led him to do strange things, such as not recognizing people. Again the shaman Toro cured him, removing the peccary fur and bird feathers causing the defect in his sight. He suffered various other attacks by animal spirits during his lifetime. In one of his accounts he told me that the shaking in one of his hands was due to them. One day, when he shot at a snake in a tree, thinking it was a capuchin monkey, he returned home sick. Nobody knew what was wrong. After a few days, his belly now heavily swollen, they took him to the hospital in Guajará where he was operated on by a physician. As he was recuperating in the Casa do Índio (Indian Infirmary) in the city, three shamans went to see him. It was one of them, Xowa, who made the diagnosis—Paletó was transforming into a snake, various parts of his body having been pierced by arrows from the snake in the tree. The shamans removed the red annatto seeds and the babassu palm oil from Paletó's body that a snake, a human being, uses to adorn himself and showed them to him. They saw his body wrapped in snakeskin, confirming his transformation into the animal. He then realized: "I'm transforming into a strange animal!" Wan e', a peccary-shaman, said that he should become a shaman and start to follow the snakes, but Wem Karamain, a trahira-fish-shaman, would not allow this to happen under any circumstances: "We're not going to let my brother suffer! Let's remove all traces of the snake from his body!" Finally, the shamans anointed his entire body and he was healed. The prophecy of Toro, who cured him when he was a boy, was realized. In curing him, he said: "You're going to live, you'll continue to live even after I die."

Paletó recounted that he may have grown to the point of crawling in Mapat, as they probably spent a year there, which was sufficient time for the stored maize to be used up, and then they left for another locality. In these relocations, not all the inhabitants traveled together. Some of them might decide to accompany other kin and head in other directions, meeting up again later in a new village or visiting each other in the interim to drink *chicha* and dance. Paletó taught me that the Wari' were always moving about, going from one place to another. Judging by my own experience trekking with them, each of these journeys would last from two to three days. They were in no hurry, since the days in the forest were spent hunting, collecting honey, and gathering fruit.

This not only applied when traveling from one village to another. As soon as they planted the maize, around September, with the rainy season beginning, all the inhabitants abandoned the plantations, spending around two months in the forest. This was the "flight from the maize," since the latter, possessing its own will, could not be observed growing or it would cease to do so. They would leave with everything they had until somebody was sent back to check on the height of the maize and then return to give their report. Before arriving, the women had to bathe; if the maize smelled them approaching, it might wither.

From Mapat, Paletó's group crossed the river called Igarapé da Gruta and arrived at Pin Karam, traversing the river again the following year when they went to Xi Kam Araji. Paletó remembers being carried in a vine sling by his mother, who used a stick to help her walk. From there they headed to the headwaters of the Igarapé Santo André and settled in Mana To', where, according to Paletó, he had already grown enough to walk and learn about things. Comparing his presumed size with one of Abrão's sons, we calculated that he would have been around three years old. We were probably in the second half of the 1930s.

6.
THE FIRST WHITE AND OTHER WARS

IT WAS IN MANA TO' that Paletó first saw a White person—or more exactly, an arm and a leg of a White man, a rubber tapper, whom his father had helped kill with arrows on the Pacaás Novos River. After most of the neighboring Indigenous groups had been exterminated by the Whites, the Whites became the main enemy of the Wari', and the most violent enemy that the Wari' had ever known. The Wari' then lived in a constant state of war, a condition that intensified in the 1940s with the arrival of a new wave of rubber tappers in their lands, who attacked them using rifles and machine guns.

Once attacked, the Wari' were initially saddened, and later, becoming angry, took revenge, killing any Whites who crossed their path. Sometimes the raids on the houses of rubber tappers also involved a search for metal tools, while leaving food, clothing, and hammocks untouched. Paletó told me that one day, encountering a dog, they killed and ate it. He laughed at my astonishment, saying that he had eaten more than one dog and that dogs tasted good.

It was not always possible to carry away parts of the dead enemy, if the Wari' were pursued and had to escape quickly.

But it was always preferred, when they could, to take some of the remains, allowing them to show it to those in the village. Most often, they took the head, the arms up to the shoulders, and the legs below the knees. The torso was left intact. Too heavy, they would say. Sometimes they cut off the scrotum and the penis to show the women, and then discarded them because such parts were never eaten.

On that specific day, as always happened when warriors returned to the village, one of the men shouted: "The warriors killed an enemy! The warriors killed an enemy! Let's cut him up! The enemy's meat has arrived with the warriors!" Paletó's father called him out so that he could shoot the enemy. Still a boy, Paletó took his small bow and a little arrow, and pierced the enemy's fingers, which were protruding from the basket used to carry the members. Others came and shot arrows too, including those adult men who had stayed at home.

Paletó remembers that the women, fearful of the enemy even when dead, left the scene, claiming that they needed to go into the forest to urinate or defecate. The men looked after the roasting. Paletó's father, probably one of the war expedition's leaders, said to the others: "Roast my prey!" They chopped firewood, assembled a grill, and in this particular instance, placed the arm and leg over the fire. Then something strange happened, which, according to Paletó, was common when roasting an enemy. First, the arm twitched and fell off onto the ground. They put it back with the help of a stick. Next the leg fell.

Once roasted, the enemy was eaten by those men who had not gone on the expedition. Sometimes, an undaunted woman would also eat. People would eat the enemy very differently from the way they ate the flesh of a dead Wari'. The enemy was eaten angrily, the flesh torn straight from the bones, as done with animal prey. Killing the enemy was an act of revenge for a death inflicted on a Wari'.

Although he did not eat because he was still small, Paletó recounted that the enemy killed by his father had fatty flesh, which was the principal quality of a prey. The bones were not burned like those of the Wari' dead, but thrown away in the forest, like those of game. The warriors did not eat the enemy because they carried his blood in their body, which would fatten them after three to four months of seclusion. During this time they drank only maize *chicha* and avoided moving about. It was such a desired state that the Wari' said they killed enemies in order to become fat, or to fatten their women, which would occur at the end of the seclusion when the ban on sexual relations was lifted.

This was the only moment when the Wari' lay in hammocks. Their hammocks were made of stretched vines, suspended from each end, and lined with mats. Two or three warriors lay on each. They would climb out of these hammocks only to receive the *chicha* offered by their kin and wives through a leaf screen that surrounded the house they were inhabiting. The women could not be seen so as not to awaken their sexual desire, which, if satisfied, would prevent them from fattening. But the young men did not give up sex so easily. Paletó recounted that, when older, he learned that this interdiction on sex during seclusion could be circumvented by placing a dead scorpion between your body and the woman's. His father, though, was less careful: on an expedition to kill enemies, he was the only one of the warriors not to fatten, because he did not resist having sex.

The warriors also climbed out of the hammocks to dance, clutching under their arms a small mat decorated with two macaw feathers long enough to appear above their heads, and playing a small flute made from bamboo with a small, pierced palm fruit on the end. Everyone recalls that they were filled with pride and self-admiration during this period. They emerged from seclusion in a beautiful state, not only because they were fat but also because they had shoulder-length hair, a style exclusive to warriors. Women competed over them and the men had sex so often that they soon became thin.

Many differences exist between the war of the Wari' and our own. Among other things, unlike the Whites who killed as many people as possible, for the Wari' one dead enemy was sufficient both for their revenge and for the constitution of men as warriors—a status also acquired by all those who shot arrows into the body of the dead enemy, or even a piece of him or her, back in the village.

Even after so-called "pacification" and until recently, the Whites were generically called by the term enemy, *wijam*. Although the Wari' no longer waged war with them, it persisted as a specter and as a possible future. When I first arrived, they referred to me as "enemy" or "wife of the enemy." But as I began to make kin among them, my position started varying from day to day: when I ate larvae, I turned into Wari'; when I stumbled over their language or forgot certain words, I was an enemy again. When I once observed, jokingly, as the elders did, that the young people were turning White, referring to their clothes, musical tastes, and use of language, my sister and namesake, To'o Orowak, the daughter of Wan e', immediately retorted: "If we had tails! We are Wari'! Only what they say may sound strange," referring to the Portuguese words frequently used by the young people. On another occasion, in Rio, I asked Paletó why he had come to refer to the inhabitants of my city as *wari'* rather than *wijam*, White, enemy. "If they were animals!" he replied.

7.

THE STONE AXE, THE DREAM OF PARIS, AND THE BACHELOR HOUSE

FROM MANA TO', Paletó's family traveled a little farther, to Terem Matam, close to the area inhabited by the OroAt territorial group, Paletó's paternal kin. By this time, Paletó was able to recognize people and already knew how to shoot small animals, which he would take home to eat. He had grown. From there they moved in succession to Hwet Pe Maku, Jein Ka Komerem, Tak Wiowio, and Koromija Kao' Wijam, heading toward the source of the Ocaia River.

They were close to an important site called Kit, in the land of the OroEo territorial group, located on the upper course of the Negro River. Kit means stone axe, and the name derives from the fact that this was the only place where the required stones for axes could be found. Many people came from all the different Wari' settlements, some of them having walked for days. On arrival, the visitors headed to the inhabitants of the village and asked to be taken to the place where the stones were found, either loose on the surface or in pits. They would hoist a large stone on their back, and then smash it by allowing it to drop to the ground. It was the smaller pieces that interested them and with which they filled their baskets to take back home. There the stones would be polished, sharpened, and attached to handles. At Kit they also found the resin used to glue the stone to the wooden handle. Grateful, they left presents for the local residents such as pots, arrows, and feathers. Sometimes they also arrived to dance and hold a festival. Collecting stones then became a less important matter, postponed until after the festival.

I went to Kit in 2002. It was a big expedition, organized with the aim of visiting this region, an area to which the Wari' had not returned since peaceful contact with the Whites, which occurred there in May 1961. We were a large group, composed mostly of men from the OroEo group, people who had been born in the Kit region. We left the Rio Negro-Ocaia Post in two canoes with small outboard motors. One of the motors belonged to my brother Abrão, and the other to our brother-in-law Orowao Kun. We slept the first night in Ocaia II village, built at the site known as Barracão Velho, which in the 1960s comprised a base for the pacification team of the Indian Protection Service (SPI), the predecessor of Funai. The other three nights we camped in the forest.

I always admired the speed with which the Wari' could turn an area of forest into a place of shelter. They would clear the ground and pad it with banana or palm leaves, tie up their square mosquito nets to tree branches, make a fire to roast the fish or game caught on the journey, eat, and go to sleep. Beth Conklin, my anthropologist *comadre*, and I had taken a two-person camping tent, and the Wari' kindly helped us assemble it. We awoke to the sounds of people packing and had to take the tent down hurriedly to continue the journey. For them, it was enough to untie and fold up the mosquito net.

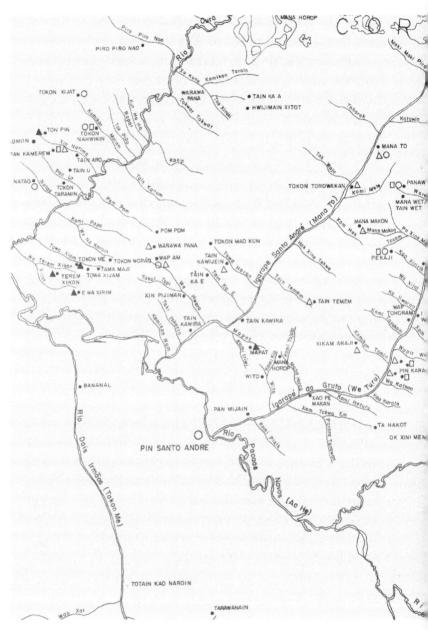

Paletó's villages

But all this haste to reach our destination was forgotten as soon as they saw the chance to hunt. They would moor the canoes and run off through the forest. Very often it was the women who encouraged the men to do so. Trekking in the forest, the women spent the whole time on the lookout for fruit trees but also trying to spot game tracks. One morning, while we were heading back home in the canoes, my sister Orowao Karaxu said she could smell peccary. The boats were full of roasted game, and the men initially ignored her comments. But she was so insistent that they stopped on the shores to search for tracks of the animals, which they did indeed find. The men then ran off with their rifles, leaving all of us women in the canoes waiting for the hunters to return with the prey.

One evening after a day's successful hunting, my brother Abrão prepared a delicacy for me: peccary liver, fried in the butter Beth and I had brought. The soft meat dissolved in the mouth and, thinking of it now, was reminiscent of foie gras. Perhaps this pleasure had set me up for the dream I jotted down in my notebook the next morning, after a night on a wooden floor full of protuberances, which left me with a sore back: I was in Paris, and glimpsed, through the windows, people lying on all kinds of mattresses, layered one on top of the other, in piles. The savory pleasure led me to dream of the sensory paradise of soft mattresses and the native land of the livers of fattened geese.

Sitting side by side for hours in the motorized canoe, I chatted at length with my sister Orowao. I learned about the infusions the women drank to alleviate menstruation and produce less blood, one of them made from maize silk. Surprised, I also discovered that Orowao was unaware whether she had wrinkles or not because she did not look in the mirror. Indeed, it is surprisingly difficult to find a mirror in the Wari' houses, and once, having searched for a long time, I eventually discovered a small piece of mirror stored in a house. Wise women.

In a nighttime conversation, lying under the full moon on the shores of the Negro River, Pelé, a young man, asked me whether the Whites had already stepped on the sun, as they had done on the moon. After Abrão explained that the moon is like a solar panel, storing the light of the sun, A'ain Xit told us about the mythic brothers Sun and Moon. The conversation turned to satellites and astronauts, and they were surprised when Beth told them that astronauts, were they to drift loose in space, would die and remain forever floating. They immediately wanted to know if they would rot. My sister Orowao added, laughing, that she would never drink rainwater again, since it might contain rotten liquid from dead astronauts. The theme of the sky and night led me to realize that when narrating a past event, the Wari' specify the period of the night concerned by pointing to the part of the sky where the sun would be during the hour of day equivalent to the hour of night in question, adding, "The image of the sun was there."

It was May and the Negro River was almost dry, especially on its higher course where we were heading. Orowao Kun, my brother-in-law, Orowao's husband, is from the OroEo territorial group and had lived in Kit when younger. He acted as our guide. Various times we had to stop and continue the river journey on foot while the men carried the canoes and motors. On the eve of our arrival in Kit, we had to abandon the canoes altogether and continue on foot for some hours, sleeping in another encampment. Very early the following day we arrived.

For me it was thrilling to arrive at Kit, having heard about the place for so many years. The landscape was formed by tall forest, with almost no trees of intermediate size, and clear forest floor underneath. We soon encountered fragments of clay pots and many axe stones on the ground, already sharpened, as though thrown away. They had probably detached from the handle or broken off, which happened frequently according to the Wari', a fact that explained their fascination with the metal axes of the Whites. To hear the area called a garden seemed odd, since it looked like a forest. Garden, though, is the name given to every locality once inhabited by the Wari', and where certain secondary forest species can be found—palms like babassu, licuri, stilt, and murumuru—along with other cultivated species like cacao and wild lemon, whose spines were used to pierce young men's ears. Only an area of primary forest, without any sign of past occupation, is called forest.

It was in Tak Wiowio, west of Kit, that Paletó moved from his parents' house to the house of bachelors, called *kaxa'*. This was a house like the others, with a stilt palm platform raised above ground, open at the sides and covered with a single-pitched roof thatched with palm leaves. The roof sloped down to the ground, forming a wall at the back of the house, precisely where a long wooden trunk was placed to serve as a pillow. In the family houses, this floor was covered by mats on which the husband and wife would lie with the children in the middle. Sometimes there would be more than one family per house. When men had two wives, as was common then, including Paletó himself for a while, the man would sleep in the middle and a wife on either side, with the respective children between them. The *kaxa'* differed by having no mats since there were no women sleeping there to weave them. The bachelors lay directly on the stilt palm, with their heads resting on the wooden trunk, and since the platform was short, as in family houses, their knees dangled from the edge of the platform, their feet hanging down. There was always a fire under the platform, which warmed the space and kept away insects and other animals.

According to Paletó, his father told him to move to the *kaxa'* built there by Jimon Pan Tokwe, another young man who would later marry one of Paletó's sisters. I asked whether he or his mother had been saddened by him moving, thinking myself of my own son Francisco living far from me. "Not at all," he replied. All of those who grew up would go to the *kaxa'*, located just a few yards from their parents' house. Accompanying Jimon and Paletó were Hwerein Pe e', his nephew, a resident of the Rio Negro-Ocaia Post whom I knew well, and his younger brother, Wao Em', later killed by another Indigenous people in an ambush. These young men slept there, but spent the day circulating in the houses, being fed by their mothers or sisters. It was there too that the men would gather after a hunt to relate their adventures, and where they entered seclusion after a war raid, when the house would be surrounded by barriers of palm leaves to isolate them from the others, especially the women. Apart from the latter instance, however, the men's house was not prohibited to women, who could sit there and listen to the conversations whenever they wanted.

When I arrived on the Negro River in 1986, there was one house that the Wari' identified as the *kaxa'*, inhabited

by a nephew of Paletó and other unmarried young men, among them Abrão, an occasional occupant, since he also kept his hammock in his parents' house. Constructed in the style of rubber tappers' abodes with stilt palm walls and a gable roof, it was a vibrant place, with various vinyl records stuck on the wall and a record player that enlivened the forró festivals. When Luiz, the first occupant, married Isabel, the others gradually stopped frequenting the house and it was eventually abandoned. Since then, I have never seen another *kaxa'* in any Wari' village.

8.

THE JAGUAR MOTHER-IN-LAW

F ROM TAK WIOWIO, Paletó's family went to plant gardens in Tokwa Mikop, where he helped his brother-in-law, the husband of his older sister, clear the area. "Whoever lives in the *kaxa'* helps his brother-in-law to plant," Paletó told me. That was when he met To'o Xak Wa, his future wife, still a baby, in a neighboring village, where she lived with her father, Jamain To'u, and her mother, A'ain Tain.

A'ain Tain told him to hold her daughter, referring to her as "your wife." "She peed in my arms," Paletó recalls. It was common for young men still living in the *kaxa'* to be asked to hold a baby girl, sometimes soon after the birth, who would then become their future wife. Ideally, when she reached puberty, the young man would return to fetch her, consummating the marriage. Older Wari' women and men tend to refer to this "groom" or "bride" as "my first husband" or "my first wife," even if the marriage had not taken place. At this first moment, one of Paletó's older brothers told him that he should go to the forest to gather honey "for our mother-in-law," which was how brothers called each other's parents-in-law, just as the wife of one of them was called "our wife" by the others. The brother himself made a bow and arrow for Paletó to give as a present "to our father-in-law," who in turn would ask his wife to offer *chicha* to "our daughter's husbands." As they lived close by, Paletó would sometimes go to visit his parents-in-law, and remembered To'o, around seven years old, offering *chicha* to him, calling him by the kinship term "mother's brother," since Paletó and his mother-in-law were classificatory siblings; in other words, they called each other brother and sister, although they were not genealogical siblings as we would know them.

Paletó's mother-in-law was no ordinary woman, To'o told me during one of the very special days the three of us spent living together in a house with two rooms, lent to us in Sagarana village, on the Guaporé River. I stayed in one of the rooms and my parents in the other. The roof, with no ceiling, enabled us to talk between the two rooms. Frequently, though, I went to their room and lay in bed next to both of them to hear stories at night.

When To'o was around five years old, one morning, after a row, her mother went to the stream and, while there, was invited by a young man, her sister's son, who called her mother, to accompany him fishing at a spot farther on, where, he said, there was a lot of fish. The young man carried her on his back along part of the path. After a time, the mother began to hear familiar voices calling to her, saying: "It's an animal who called you! It's not a Wari'! Look, here's your daughter! She's crying a lot." The true nephew shouted at the one pretending to be him, whom everyone, save for the abducted woman, knew to be a jaguar: "Leave my mother on the ground!" That was when she realized that her supposed nephew had been licking leaves along the path, just like jaguars do. She looked carefully and saw a small length of tail. Because of her kin's insistent calling to her, the jaguar-nephew let her go and vanished. According to To'o, her mother was covered in jaguar fur after being carried. When I asked her whether her mother had feared the jaguar, To'o replied: "She wasn't afraid. It was a *wari'* [a person]!"

A short while later, they went to a festival in another settlement. To'o's father killed a woodpecker and handed it to his wife for her to cook. Unintentionally, To'o's mother touched her mouth with her dirty fingers, swallowing the blood. This made her a commensal of the jaguars, who eat raw meat. At night, her mother was in their house, built in the old style without walls. She was sleeping on the stilt palm platform with her daughter To'o in one arm and a nephew in the other, when a jaguar leaped on top of her and dragged her into the forest by her arms, until it bumped into a tree trunk and fled, pursued by the Wari'. She was bleeding heavily and had jaguar claw marks all over her body. They took care of her and treated her with maize smoke, used by the Wari' to drive away the doubles of animals. She was healed of her injuries.

Some time later, by now living in another locality, To'o's father killed many capuchin monkeys in the forest. According to To'o, her mother acted as if she already knew what her father had caught and went to the forest to meet him. Seeing the prey, she bit the neck of a monkey, still raw, and drank its blood. She then quickly spat it out. But what To'o and other people saw emerge from her mouth was not blood but leftovers of maize *chicha*. For the Wari', what they see as blood, the jaguar sees as *chicha*. Having become identified with the jaguars, To'o's mother had started to have two bodies simultaneously, one human, the other animal. She was now capable of a very particular kind of translation: rather than substituting one word for another, as our translators do, she transformed one thing into another within her body. One time, To'o's mother called to her daughters to come bathe in the river. There were many small leporinus fish visible swimming about. She then said to the girls: "I'm going to fetch insect larvae. Sew up some leaves so we can roast them." Meanwhile, she caught the small fish. Yet when she showed them to her daughters, they were not fish, they were insect larvae. Narrating the event to me, To'o exclaimed: "The fish all turned into larvae!" On another occasion, To'o went to the forest with her mother and older sister. They made a straw basket and, on the river, caught many pimelodella, another type of small fish. Their mother swallowed them raw and spat out bits of patawa palm *chicha*. On seeing this, people exclaimed: "They were fish! They all turned into patawa!" It was during this period that To'o's mother started to cure sick people, becoming one of the few Wari' women to act as a shaman.

Sitting next to us during this account, Paletó added that his mother-in-law was born strange, with one tooth. As commonly happens with shamans, whose partnerships and thus bodies vary during their lifetime, To'o's mother at a certain point ceased to accompany the jaguars and began to follow the capuchin monkeys and later the agoutis. Paletó also recalled that To'o's grandmother, her father's mother, had been a shaman. In other words, there had been a particular family partnership with the animals. To'o's mother died many years later due to the epidemics that followed contact with the Whites. Paletó recounted that they had buried her body (as they used to do with people who died from diseases of foreign origin) but after a few days she was no longer there. "Perhaps it had been removed by a giant armadillo," he told me.

Although I knew about these abductions by jaguars, which took place until the recent past, I had never been given a detailed account from someone so close. The most recent case, which I only heard through secondhand accounts, had involved Marcos, a young adult from the Negro River, who had been called by a jaguar pretending to be an employer of SUCAM, then the public sanitation and health company for the Amazon. Noticing my interest in these cases, To'o took me to a house neighboring our own in Sagarana, inhabited by a woman of around sixty years who herself had been abducted by a jaguar.

Paletó, To'o, and I sat down on the cement floor of her home, in an area with a television at the back. Next to us sat some of the woman's grandchildren, as well as other people who arrived out of curiosity. We chatted politely until I explained to her the episode that I wanted to hear and record. By the time I placed my small microphone on her clothing and switched on the recorder, quite a lot of people had gathered around us.

When the event happened, she had been around five years old. One day, the adults sent the children to the river to fetch water. This was when her mother appeared and called her for them to catch fish in another spot. She went along. She did not know it was a jaguar, since it was exactly like her mother. On the path they encountered fruits from a palm tree much relished by the Wari', and her mother removed maize from the basket she was carrying for them to eat with the fruit.

Shortly after a thorn became stuck in the child's foot, which her mother pulled out. At this point, the listeners laughed in surprise, marveling at the jaguar's very human gesture. After walking for a while, they stopped to sleep. Milk was seeping from the mother's breast since she was feeding a baby at the time. When the girl was almost asleep, she perceived a man approach. He lay on top of the mother to have sex. The girl asked: "Who is this man?" The mother smacked her buttocks lightly a few times. Again the listeners laughed, and Paletó explained to me that mothers do this at night when their children awake. The next day, they ate the palm fruit and carried on walking, until the girl heard the voice of her older brother calling her. At this moment, the supposed mother said that she was going to defecate and vanished into the forest. Her kin then approached. The girl's body was covered in jaguar fur, which they cleaned off. At the end of the narrative, I asked whether she had not seen any trace of jaguar in the supposed mother, a bit of tail or something similar, to which she responded: "Nothing. It truly was my mother."

According to the Wari', jaguars had a "heart," though, and thus when an abducted person's kin arrived, they would release the victim and depart. As To'o explained to me: "Jaguars are true people," in the moral sense. The same does not apply to tapirs, who when they take someone do not allow the victim to return. Paletó and To'o witnessed a rare case of a boy who was abducted by a tapir and returned. According to Paletó's account, one day the young man went to hunt with other men and disappeared. When they searched for him, they found his footprints following tapir tracks and concluded that the tapir had taken him. His kin cried a lot, and after some days searching, gave up trying to look for him. A long time later, trekking in the forest, some men saw him. He had a human appearance, but the knees and hands of a tapir. His body was covered in large tapir ticks and he scratched himself constantly. They removed all the ticks and he got better. But like To'o's mother, he began to act strangely. He ate leaves. One time, he took them a pile of fruits of a kind that the Wari' do not eat, claiming that they were edible. They treated him with maize smoke, and he seemed to get better. "Only his knees were like those of a tapir," Paletó said. Today, he explained, these abductions no longer occur, not because the animals are incapable or have no desire for humans, but because the forest is now distant and young people no longer go there.

Some years later Paletó told me something that I had never known: his father-in-law, Jamain To'u, was equally strange, since for a while, after killing a peccary, he began to have a double that accompanied these animals and grunted like them. This was common among men, who from time to time would be attacked by an animal double and begin to follow it. They were shamans, even if temporarily; in other words, they had "strange eyes" or "freed eyes." Already in my second month among the Wari', I wrote in my field notebook: "There seems to be many stories of people turning into animals. As though this threshold were easy to cross." Little did I realize that all my future work would be marked by this perception.

9.
THE WIVES

PALETÓ'S OLDEST BROTHER, Manim, died, leaving
behind two widows. One of them was To'o Min, the
young girl who had saved Paletó's life by running with him
into the forest as soon as he was born. She had two children
with Manim and, following the husband's death, it was the
custom for the younger brother to inherit one of his wives
and their children. Paletó began to have sex with her. She
became pregnant and had a daughter, called Pijim. Even so,
he did not want to take her as a wife. He argued that he already had a young wife—referring to To'o Xak Wa—and did
not want another. Because of his reluctance, her kin arrived
armed with war clubs, demanding that he take her with him
to his house, which act in itself consummated the marriage.

At this moment, a snake bit his older brother, and Paletó went to treat him with the smoke of agouti fur and the
feathers of various kinds of birds. These are animals that eat
snake and so are curative. As far as I know, it was not necessary to be a shaman to perform this cure, although Paletó
might have been one at that time. A month passed before
his brother was cured, and only then did Paletó go to fetch
the widow and her children for them to live with him in Pin

Karam. They then had another daughter, To'o Em, and a son, Wao Em', a name inherited from Paletó's younger brother, and later passed on to my own older son, Francisco.

Now living with the widow, her children, and their children, Paletó, encouraged by his brother, went to the village of To'o, the wife he had received as a baby, to fetch her, since she had grown up. "My wife was beautiful," he said, "with reddish hair and small breasts." The two brothers arrived where she lived with her parents. Paletó addressed his mother-in-law, whom he called sister: "I have come to fetch our daughter, my older sister. Tell her to come." The adolescent had no desire to go with him and ran off. Paletó and his brother stayed overnight and the following day Paletó insisted: "I shall take our daughter, my older sister!" "Take her!" she replied. "She's a child no longer." And turning to her daughter: "Your husband arrived!" To'o grabbed tight to one of the house posts: "I don't like him, I don't like him!" Her mother insisted: "He is your true husband, he bathed you when you were little." She packed a small basket with her daughter's things, including annatto for her to paint herself. "Go!" she said. To'o cried. "Her mother felt no pity," Paletó remarked. Eventually she set out with Paletó and his brother. About halfway along the trail, though, she ran back. "This small young woman was really scared of me!" In the end, the mother had to drag her by the ears (this episode was also narrated to me various times by To'o herself), pushing her toward Paletó.

To'o was a slender woman with an erect posture, common to Wari' women, and wore the typical hairstyle, a bob: straight and cut short at ear level, with bangs. I estimated a fifteen-year difference between the couple, considering that

Paletó was an adolescent when he had held her as a baby. But it is difficult to be more accurate than that, because as they grew older the difference in age became nearly unnoticeable. In retelling the episode of the marriage, Paletó said: "She didn't like it, she didn't like it, but afterwards she did, she became my people, we formed a pair, she followed me." One time he told me, smiling, how he painted To'o's entire body in black designs using the juice of the genipap fruit for them to attend a festival.

When I met them, they were inseparable companions, and To'o appeared fascinated with Paletó's vivacity, attentively listening to everything he said and laughing a lot at his stream of jokes. One of the times when Paletó told me how she was scared of him when she was young, I turned to To'o and, laughing, asked her whether she still felt the same: "I'm no longer afraid," she replied with a smile. Another time, Paletó, my sons, and I were driving by car to their house in Linha 29, after having spent time on the Negro River, and stopped at the house of his daughter, my sister Orowao, in Linha 26, to fetch To'o, who had been living there for a couple of months. On seeing the car, she ran to us, visibly full of longing, and asked, "Where is Paletó? Where is Paletó?" She was relieved to see him. I remember this moment very clearly because immediately afterward, before entering the car to continue the journey with us, To'o went back into the house and brought out two mats woven by her to give to Francisco, who had declared his wish, some time earlier, to sleep on mats. He did so for years after we returned to Rio.

Paletó and To'o always sat close to one another, with their legs touching. From time to time she would concentrate on picking his nits, removing ticks from his hands and feet, and

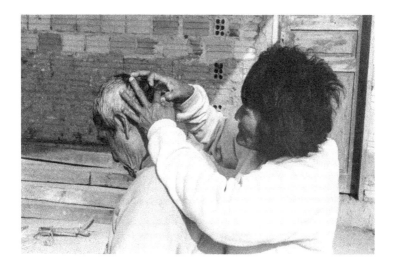

scratching his back. She had cared for him with affection ever since his movements started to become limited, and played a crucial role during the event that could have led to his death. To'o told me that when Wan e', my shaman father, was already extremely sick, he called Paletó to go with him to drink *chicha* underwater—that is, for him to accompany him in death. She intervened decisively: "Paletó stays!" After they became believers, Paletó said that To'o was truly his rib, referring to the Biblical episode of Adam and Eve.

I do not know why To'o did not become my mother completely, although I did call her mother. We were close, we talked a lot, but we both felt that something was missing between us that kept us from becoming true kin, as I had become to Paletó. Perhaps if she had visited my home in Rio de Janeiro, which never happened, she would have come to know me and my family better, and the sense that something was missing would have changed. Nonetheless, often she behaved toward me like a mother, especially when she was by Paletó's side. During the period when we lived in Sagarana, just the three of us in one house, I was once severely reprimanded by her as though I were an adolescent daughter. I had gone out late afternoon, having told them that I was going to a friends' house nearby. When I arrived at my destination, the television on the veranda was switched on, with several people watching the news program, and I sat next to them, forgetting the time, amused by the soap opera that followed, *América*, which was very popular there, especially due to one song, whose refrain, "hello cowboy crew, hello cowherd crew," was often repeated by the youths. When I returned home, To'o was waiting for me at the door, anxious, and began to speak nonstop about how concerned she and Paletó had been by my absence, especially because various non-Indigenous workers were in Sagarana at the time, constructing washbasins. According to her, they could have grabbed me on a trail and forced me to have sex, given that I was walking alone in the dark. I felt a mixture of tenderness for their concern with me and anger at being scolded, experiencing new feelings of being a daughter in that world.

As a beautiful teenager, when To'o arrived, Paletó's first wife felt jealous. She treated the young woman harshly, despite calling her sister, which is how one addresses a first-degree cousin. "She didn't want me to bring another wife, she wanted to be the only one," Paletó said to me. "Why did you bring her? You've already had lots of sex!" his wife said to him. The day after her arrival, the first wife called the younger one to go bathing with her in the river and, jealous, told Paletó not to follow them, as a husband commonly did with his wives. "I wasn't angry. Only unmarried young men get angry," he said.

To'o remained in a constant back-and-forth between her parents' house, in a nearby village, and the house of her husband, until over time she gained "'courage" in relation to Paletó and started to offer him food. She began to sleep by his side at home, Paletó lying between his two wives. Only after some time passed, Paletó recounted, did he have sex with her for the first time, in the forest, the most frequent place for sex with younger wives, while the older wives, with children, are sought by their husbands at night.

Paletó did not tell me whether he insisted that To'o have sex with him, and by his account it seems that she naturally drew closer to him. Probably the initiative to have sex the first time came from him, although, very often among the Wari', it was the women, especially lovers, who would take the initiative. In these cases, the woman would pull out the cylindrical piece of wood used as an earring by the young man, lick it, and throw it on the ground, or perhaps tickle his back. The man would then say that he had to go into the forest to cut firewood and, after a while, she would say that she was going to the forest to defecate. There they would have sex, him on top of her. Paletó told me that the women used to complain a bit about the thorns on the ground. The wives, for their part, suspected their husbands of having lovers when sexual intercourse lasted longer than usual. I was told this by a woman friend who explained to me that, in fact, they liked it when their husband ejaculated quickly.

I suspect that the perception of the growing intimacy between To'o and Paletó led the first wife to reject the young woman even more. It seems that this type of conflict was common among wives, even though they would usually be kin among themselves. To'o thus decided to return to her parents' house once more. Over time, though, the wives became close companions, helping each other in domestic tasks and looking after the children. I see now, reading my notebooks, that this situation left an impression on me. I wrote down a dream in my second month of fieldwork: "I dreamt that I was married to a guy who had three women and had to take turns sleeping one night with each of them. One was really annoying, never allowing him to be close to the others. I was the first to leave. In the end, the annoying one left too, and just one was left, Topa' Jam, one of my friends from the Negro River, in whose yard we sang and recorded the women's songs."

The solution to Paletó's matrimonial imbroglio was different from the one I dreamt. After a while, his first wife asked him to call the young wife back, and Paletó set off, once again accompanied by his brother, to fetch To'o, who this time really did not want to go. She ran off to the forest with her younger sister, claiming that the other wife was very angry with her. "It seemed like she knew that the Whites would kill her," Paletó said. By staying away, To'o escaped the massacre that was about to happen.

10.
ESCAPING DEATH FOR
THE SECOND TIME

The Massacre

I HEARD VARYING ACCOUNTS of the massacre. Each time I was deeply moved. Paletó told the episode vividly, his expression one of anger more than sadness. The account I narrate here was told to me in Rio de Janeiro, on December 17, 2012. Paletó, Abrão, and I had just spent the weekend at Itacoatiara beach in Niterói, and then continued on to another nearby beach, Camboinhas, to visit the Guarani Mbyá. My student Amanda, who also accompanied us, was conducting research with the Guarani. To get to Camboinhas, we had crossed a river on foot and returned with the water now at waist height, much to Paletó's amusement and also a certain apprehension.

Back in Rio de Janeiro, Paletó had talked at length on Skype with the missionary Barbara Kern, who, now living in Germany, had lived for many years among the Wari'. Soon after their call, I switched on the recorder and asked Paletó once again to tell his life story. He told the story of the massacre that happened in 1955 in Xi Kam Araji, a site close to the Igarapé da Gruta River, some eight hours' walk from where the Rio Negro-Ocaia Post is now located.

A few days before the massacre, Paletó and a group of men, while hunting spider monkeys on the shores of the

Pacaás Novos, saw some Whites. As they had been whistling to alert one another of the monkeys' whereabouts, Paletó infers that the Whites had heard them. The men arrived back home and advised the others. Paletó, his wife To'o Min, and the children lived in a neighboring village and were at Xi Kam Araji visiting Paletó's father and helping him host the festival. After a night filled with dancing during which the guests drank heavily, vomited, and passed out, the hosts, among them Paletó, went to douse them with lukewarm water in the morning to awaken them, and the guests then left.

As is common after the festivals, the residents went to bathe in the river very early in the morning, after their guests had left. Paletó, his wife, their daughter To'o Em, who must have been about five years old, and Wao Em', their small boy of about one, were on the trail leading from the place where the *chicha* festival had been held to the river. The daughter asked her father to carry her, but Paletó had hurt his foot stumbling on a branch while hunting the spider monkeys. He asked his wife to carry her and took little Wao Em' in his arms. Their son was not walking yet, and Paletó remembers that while carrying him on his shoulders the boy sucked his hair.

On returning from bathing, climbing up the trail toward the houses, they heard gunshots. "Tatatatata," Paletó mimicked, reminding me of the sound of machine guns. They saw that the older son of Paletó's wife, from his brother's marriage, was lying dead. Paletó's father ran along a trail close to home when, enraged, he decided to stop and turn to face the shooters, shouting: "You killed my grandson, you horrid enemies! He was my grandson, you horrid enemies!" He fell silent, shot in the chest, and collapsed to the ground. Paletó's mother managed to flee and stumble to a nearby settlement, but, having been shot in the back, died soon afterward.

Carrying their children, Paletó and his wife tried to run but a bullet struck the girl To'o Em, who fell to the ground. She shouted, "Father, father, the enemy hit me!" "How beautiful was my daughter who the Whites killed!" Paletó exclaimed to me. Clutching his small son in his arms, Paletó kept running and ended up bashing his head on a branch. Dazed, he thought he had been struck by a bullet too. The son cried out, thinking that his father was dead. His wife, seeing the daughter fallen, stopped running and decided to return, crawling over the ground to try to avoid the bullets, with an arm covering her face to protect herself. One of the shooters, perceiving that the mother had returned, ceased firing until she grabbed her daughter, and then fired at her. He shot her in the vagina, but she did not die at that moment. She just lay there.

Paletó reached the shore and crossed the river, carrying Wao Em'. On the other side, he encountered the festival guests and told them what had happened: "They killed our children and their mother!" Two of his wife's sons and Pijim, their daughter, had escaped. The men got ready to return and shoot the Whites. One by one they stood up holding their bow: Orowao Totoro, Wem Kanum, Wan Hon Tamatara— Paletó named them each on a finger. They rushed ahead, but when they got there, the Whites were no longer to be found. Paletó, arriving later, became angry, saying that they should have waited for him since he was the one who should shoot.

As they headed there, Paletó's wife, badly injured, managed to walk to a nearby village and collapsed on a stilt palm platform in one of the houses. As soon as the men arrived, she asked Paletó about their daughter's body: "Why did you leave it there?" she inquired angrily. Paletó replied that he had been forced to run with their son. The inhabitants of the house then fled, carrying his injured wife on their backs. She died on the way and they stopped. Many people arrived to cry over her, roast her, and eat her, among them Paletó's OroAt paternal kin, two of whom were the brothers Wao Tokori and Jamain Tamanain, whom I met on the Negro River. The latter is still alive today.

As well as Paletó's father, his brother's son and his own daughter, the wife of Hwerein Pe e', his nephew, with whom he had spent time living in the bachelors' house in the past, also died, along with two of his daughters, both children. Hwerein Pe e' escaped but more than once showed me the bullet scars on his back. Other inhabitants of the Negro River with visible gunshot wounds were Mo'am, sister of Hwerein Pe e', and two younger brothers of Paletó on his father's side, Xiemain and Patan.

Xiemain was then a child of around five and, hit by a bullet, ran alone into the forest and remained hidden for some days, surviving on what he managed to forage, until he was encountered by a man. Paletó observed that Xiemain had a "strange" body, since he was shot again in another attack by Whites and survived. On this occasion, two other men died.

According to Paletó, the Whites returned to Xi Kam Araji and remained there close by, keeping watch, for some days. When the Wari' finally managed to reach the bodies, they had rotted and been partially eaten by vultures. The Whites had stuck two arrows through Paletó's father's mouth. Even so, the Wari' took what remained of the bodies, and Paletó was able to see the foot of his daughter To'o Em, the only part of her body still intact. The rotting remains were placed in baskets and taken to a village on the other shore of the river, where they were roasted, one of the grills covered solely by the bodies of children. Fleeing, they continued farther still until finally they could stop to eat the dead.

In July 2007, accompanied by the anthropologist Beth Conklin and the archaeologist Dusan Boric, we visited Xi Kam Araji, the location of the massacre, with some Wari' men and women, who returned there for the first time in fifty years. Paletó was unable to go with us since the two-day walk would have been difficult for him. It was no easy walk. After an hour by tractor and several more hours trekking, we took around three hours to cross the Igarapé da Gruta River on foot. While the Wari', barefoot, waded easily through the water at knee height, we, the foreigners, felt our boots filling with water and mud, and were forced to remove them and walk barefoot on the river bottom as they did. Dusan took a photo of Beth and me with water at thigh-height, each of us holding onto a long stick with our boots tied at the top like flags. I had a terrible fear of hurting my foot in that desolate place and being unable to walk further, since we had no idea where we were stepping. What might lie underneath? Walking on, we found, on a rock, a dead young caiman, and I immediately imagined its mother lurking nearby. Nothing happened, but on the return, at the suggestion of our archaeologist, who always had good ideas for this type of situation, we swapped the boots for flip-flops, covered by socks, and wrapped in silver tape. At first, we were able to walk without a problem, but soon enough, the tape began to come unstuck, our socks became waterlogged, and we had to remove the flip-flops and carry on barefoot as we had done before. The next day, at the Sunday church service, the pastor Awo Kamip, Paletó's nephew and our companion on the trek, describing the trip to those present, observed that we, the Whites, had very thin skin on our feet.

A'ain Kaxun, Paletó's half-brother on his father's side, present at the massacre, was one of our guides. Arriving at the site, he told me that his eyes were welling up. He showed me the places of each of the houses and the spot where his father had been shot. The pillars of some houses were still standing and could be seen amid the forest growing around them. We saw bullet marks in trees and shards of pots shattered by bullets. That was when I learned that my other father, Wan e', and my mother Orowao Xik Waje, had also been living there at the time, and managed to flee with their three small children. The video that we made at the location, with some people relating the massacre, was shown on the same day as our return, on a television set turned to face the area outside one of the houses.

While we were staying in Xi Kam Araji, the pastor Awo Kamip recalled that when he was about seven years old, in another of these armed attacks, his father had been killed and had one of his ears sliced off by a White man. I heard many other accounts of massacres during my time living with them. One such episode was told to me by a man from the OroMon group, during an expedition that I undertook, accompanied by Paletó and To'o, to this group's territory in 2003. He was between seven and eight years old when the event happened, suggesting it must have been around 1960. He recalls that the Whites threw the dead Wari' children in the air so that they fell on the machetes and were cut in two. According to the emeritus bishop Dom Roberto, who told me the exact same details when we conversed about the massacres, these scenes of horror were commonplace.

The peace that supposedly governs the relation between the Wari' and Whites today is highly tenuous, with tensions flaring up on occasion. In urban commerce, the Wari' are stigmatized for their appearance and their difficulty in speaking Portuguese. On some recent occasions, rubber tappers have entered Wari' villages situated on the edge of their territory at night and threatened them at gunpoint, causing so much panic that one of the villages, Ocaia II, was abandoned. In July 2005, when the boat pilot Chagas, Paletó, To'o, and I were at the Guajará-Mirim port, already on board set to leave for Sagarana, we were approached by armed soldiers, part of a border patrol operation. Paletó and To'o remained immobile, crouched and completely silent while we spoke with the soldiers. They were terrified. When finally we obtained the life jackets we needed and left, Paletó said that God had helped us, precisely as he had helped Moses, also imprisoned by soldiers and assisted by God.

In response to these aggressions, the Wari', before they became Christians, would always seek revenge, even when, after contact, the massive presence of Whites in the surrounding region made war unfeasible. The shamans told me that White people from the city thought that they died from everyday diseases, but in fact they had been attacked by Wari' shamans. Those who thought that someone had died from a jaguar attack did not know that the jaguar was the double of a shaman, who had attacked the White person on purpose, as in a war. Orowam, the jaguar-shaman from the Negro River, related to me various episodes of attacks on White people by his animal body. As well as shamans, Wari' young men in the

1980s dreamed about joining the army, which was difficult to do since they lacked the necessary school qualifications. Those who did enlist often ended up deserting, unhappy with the excessive work and discipline. But when I asked them why they had insisted on pursuing a military career, they unhesitatingly replied: "To kill White people!"

11.
THE BEWITCHED BRIDE AND POISON IN THE HOUSES

AROUND THE TIME of the massacre, To'o, Paletó's young wife, or bride on the run, had become sick and was very thin. "She almost died," he said, explaining that the disease had been caused by sorcery. A sorcerer, probably a man, had assembled a small wooden rack in the distant forest, decorating it with annatto and white plumes so that it was beautiful and attractive. On it he had placed something that To'o liked a lot, perhaps honey or the meat of a favorite game animal. If it were today, he might place a mosquito net, clothing, or even money. The sorcerer then dug a hole in the ground or close to water and, at night, blew into the hole, whispering: "To'o, To'o Xak Wa!"

Sleeping, To'o began to dream of the presents being offered to her and replied to the call saying *ha!* (hi!). Her double, appearing as a baby, pale-skinned and slippery, went to meet the sorcerer and was immediately tied up by him with vines on the wooden rack, in a fetal position. The sorcerer began to torture the small white To'o, poking her with small sticks or arrow tips. Meanwhile, she, at home, her body rigid, adopted the same fetal position of her double. As sudden deaths are very often attributed to sorcery, sorcerers avoid targeting the heart initially to confuse others about the cause of death and avert suspicion. As a result, in To'o's case there was time for shamans to intervene. They removed the images of the sticks and arrows from her body at home, while their animal bodies, walking in the forest, found the rack and untied the double of To'o. She did not know the identity of the sorcerer; because he acted only at night, it had not been possible to see his face in her dream.

I saw a woman bewitched only one time, at the end of 1986. She had been taken to the Casa do Índio (Indian Infirmary) in Guajará-Mirim, where I met her. I was struck by the rigidity of her body, coiled in a fetal position. People tried hard to stretch out her limbs but failed. Multiple shamans performed cures, removing small sticks and arrow tips from her, which they then showed everyone else. They also said that there were all kinds of animals in her body. Another woman, telling me about the death throes of her father, killed by sorcery, said that his body seeped honey, which indicated that the honey had been used to lure the victim's double. The woman in Guajará-Mirim was eventually cured and, just like To'o, had been unable to see the sorcerer's face.

Jao was someone I knew who was killed by sorcery, though I did not see him die. Paletó recounted that after a fight with war clubs, initiated over a suspected case of adultery in the neighboring village of Santo André, men from the Negro River had gone to Santo André in retaliation. A relative of Jao's wife who lived there had been struck on the head with a club by Jao's relatives, which led the injured man to assemble a wooden rack and call Jao's double, offering him a beautiful woman. Jao woke up saying that he had dreamed of spirits, went to the river, and already had a fever by the time he returned. He died rapidly. A thorn had been stuck in his throat, which had swollen up. Orowam, a jaguar-shaman, told me at the time that, walking in the forest with his animal body, he encountered the rack that had been made to kill Jao, but it was too late. On another occasion, however, he managed to save Awo Kamip, who had dreamed of an armadillo offered to him by the sorcerer. When jaguar-Orowam appeared, he fled. Another victim was A'ain's father. According to Paletó, he had arrows in each of his eyes, a babassu stick coming out of his thigh and peach palm out of his chest. They were not images of sticks, which only a shaman could see, but actual sticks, visible to everyone.

To'o, the bride on the run, having survived the sorcery attack, finally agreed to the marriage, arriving to raise Paletó's orphaned children and breastfeed little Wao Em'. Her breasts were full of milk as her child conceived with Paletó had aborted when she had taken refuge in her parents' house and become sick. Pijim, Paletó's daughter with his first wife, To'o Min, went with her older sister to live with her paternal OroAt kin and, taking sick, ended up dying there. From Paletó's children there remained Wem Parawan, actually his deceased brother's son, already a young man, as well as Wao Em', who was being breastfed by To'o. According to Paletó, To'o adopted the two and thought of them as her own sons, and she was extremely upset when told that Wem Parawan had died from sorcery at the place called Ton Kat.

The motive for the sorcery was adultery. A man from the OroEo territorial group accused the young man of having had sex with his wife, and it is likely that he had been the sorcerer. Their relatives went to summon Paletó and To'o, saying: "The OroEo killed your son!" By the time the victim's relatives arrived, the dead body had already swollen up and it could be seen that he had been skewered with many sticks. Hornets emerged from his mouth and his body was covered in bites, a sign that the sorcerer had used a hornets' nest as a vehicle to call the name of the deceased and attract his double.

To'o, her breasts full of milk, sobbed heavily, Paletó told me. In revenge, one of Paletó's kin arranged a visit to the village of the kin of the presumed sorcerer with the plan of hiding a poisonous vine, called *paparato*, in the wall of one of the houses. The inhabitants began to fall sick and inferred that they had been poisoned by the OroNao', people from Paletó's family, and searched for the vine. Having found it, they threw it in the water, but not before two people had died. The poison then, taken by the water, returned in the direction of the OroNao', killing some people, among them one of the sons of my peccary-father Wan e'. Some years later, Wao Em', Paletó's younger son, whom To'o had breastfed, sickened and died.

Soon after, To'o became pregnant with Orowao Karaxu, her first daughter, who was born at the place called Kaxima, probably between 1958 and 1959.

12.
MEETING THE WHITES

I T WAS 1961, the month of May. The situation in the region around Guajará-Mirim had been tense for almost a decade, ever since rubber tappers had decided to advance even further into Wari' lands, leading to massacres like the one involving Paletó's family. Whenever they could, the Wari' took revenge, killing Whites. There reached a point, however, when the violence of the Whites was such that the Wari' began to flee toward ever more inaccessible places, like the lands of the OroEo and OroAt territorial groups, along the upper course of the Negro and Ocaia Rivers, the territory in which Paletó was living at that moment, having moved from Ton Kat to Hwijimain Xitot. Not far from there, Koxain was the place chosen by the so-called pacification team to contact the Wari'.

This team was composed of a Catholic priest, Father Roberto Arruda, whom I would later meet in Guajará, by then an emeritus bishop; Fernando Cruz, an employee of the Indian Protection Service (SPI); Gilberto Gama, also of the SPI, who arrived later; Rui Figueiredo, from the *Diários Associados* newspaper group; Saul, a member of the Kanoê Indigenous people; and some other non-Indigenous men recruited in Guajará. Accompanying them too were various Wari' men from groups previously contacted by American Evangelical missionaries from the New Tribes Mission, who had arrived in the region at the end of the 1940s with the express aim of making contact. After many attempts, the missionaries had succeeded in establishing peaceful contact with the Wari' population that had spent fifty years isolated from the rest, mostly people from the OroNao' territorial group, the same as Paletó's, living on the feeder rivers of the left shore of the Pacaás Novos.

According to the Wari' themselves, their isolation had been caused by heavy rains and the sudden broadening of the river, which enabled an increase in the boat traffic of the Whites. This, in turn, prevented the Wari' from traversing between the shores, a crossing previously achieved easily on foot during the dry season. The first contacts occurred in 1956, exclusively with this population, and only five years later, in April 1961, did the same missionaries successfully approach another segment of the population, formed by the OroMon, OroWaram, and OroWaramXijein territorial groups, who lived on the right shore of the Laje, not far from the Madeira-Mamoré Railway. These people—both the ones contacted five years earlier and the ones contacted only a month previously—were recruited for the expedition to the Negro River. Given the rivalry with the priests, the Evangelical missionaries were excluded from the new expedition and resented the fact they were not even informed that it had been organized.

The team arrived in Koxain village, which was empty, and hung up metal axes and machetes on the house posts. Jimon Pan Tokwe lived in the neighboring locality of Terem Matam and still had a maize crop in Koxain. One day when he went to harvest the maize, he saw the tools on the posts, grabbed them, and took them back to his kin in Terem Matam. They were amazed by the stupidity of the Whites, leaving the tools so openly on show. "The Whites aren't thinking straight, they're fools!" they remarked. They returned the next day to find more. The news traveled upriver, where Paletó lived, and they began to ponder whether they should go there to shoot these foolish Whites. They decided to travel downriver in the direction of Koxain, which was in fact the way to their own lands situated in the territory of the OroNao', which they had abandoned due to fear of White attacks.

Paletó recounts that he was accompanied by his father-in-law, some other men, and their wives. On the path, they saw an armadillo hole and waited for nightfall to kill it. They roasted and ate the animal. "Let's shoot the Whites so they don't enter our houses! Let's go!" When they arrived at Terem Matam, they discovered that other men, among them Paletó's younger brother and his nephew A'ain—the man who one day appeared at my house early in the morning to take me to stay outside the village, in Ta' Nakot, for the first time—had already gone to Koxain to shoot the Whites. "They should have waited for us!" they complained.

Meanwhile, the warriors were spying on the encampment of those whom they had decided were a band of foolish Whites, seemingly waiting to be shot on the opposing shore, downriver on the Ocaia. Judging by the sounds, they appeared to be building a shelter, but they were surprised by the whistle of the white-throated tinamou, which the Wari' imitate to call one another. They were astonished: "The Whites know how to whistle like the white-throated tinamou!" Then they heard these Whites speak to each other in the Wari' language, which surprised them further still. "The Whites know how to speak!" In fact, it was the Wari' from the expedition chatting to each other, but they did not look Wari': they wore clothes and had short hair. The warriors retreated. Paletó added: "We were really scared of the Whites, daughter! We thought they'd kill us!"

The warriors slept, and the next morning they saw a canoe approaching along the Ocaia from where the Whites were camped. Paletó's brother called his nephew A'ain: "Let's go, let's shoot the Whites!" In the prow of the passing canoe was a clothed man and, behind him, a man without a shirt, whom they chose to shoot. The two men drew their bows at the same time, but just as they released the string, their arms touched and instead of striking the man's chest, they hit his arm. He fell in the water, yelling. The one in the prow of the canoe jumped in the water too, shouting in the Wari' language: "You shot the White man! It's us, OroNao'." But the warriors had already run far off.

One of the warriors, Jimon Pan Tokwe, headed in another direction, toward Koxain, the place where the tools had been hung up and where he had planted his maize crop. He was walking on the path when he encountered a man. "Father," the man said, "you shot one of us [referring to the White man injured in the canoe]!" Jimon recognized him—the man had been there only a short while ago as a guest at a festival. He was his kin, from the OroMon territorial group, who had been contacted a month earlier and joined the team of the Whites. "Father, they arrived at the OroMon and we went toward the Whites! You shot Joaquim, a White man. The one in the prow rowing was Xijan!" The other Wari' then arrived, those who had been isolated fifty years earlier on the far shore of the Pacaás Novos. "It's us," they said, but Jimon did not recognize them, since they had never met. Jimon asked about an aunt who, he knew, had crossed to the other shore. "She died," they said, "but all your nephews are alive." They gave Jimon axes and machetes and headed off together to Terem Matam, where his people lived.

I try to imagine Jimon, whom I met as an older man on the Negro River, when he was young and active. When I met him he was a tall and slender man with close-cropped hair. He had had three wives, but when we met, he was a widower and lived in a very small house, alongside the house of his married daughter. One of his grandsons, of unusually small stature (I only heard of one other such case among the Wari', a young woman), lived with him, keeping him company. As men do not tend cooking fires, a female task, I saw Jimon various times bring lots of fish and leave them next to a log fire without anyone approaching to roast them. Perhaps hungry, he would wander around nearby, without asking for anything, until one of his granddaughters decided to tend the fire. At the time of this contact expedition, his wives were alive, and there was no lack of cooking fires.

Xiemain, Paletó's younger brother, the one who had evaded the bullets in the massacre, was still a boy and, on seeing the newly arrived Wari', was certain they were not Indigenous and called them enemies. One of these men explained to the child: "We're Wari'. We cut our hair, that's all!" And each of them said his name, demonstrating that they were Wari' names. The people from the house remained unconvinced. They drew their bows: "Let's shoot the enemies!" At the same time, Paletó's group arrived along the path also ready to shoot their arrows. They saw them and shouted: "Don't shoot us, we're not enemies, we're Wari', we're OroNao'. The Whites found us, and we went toward them. The OroMon too. Only you here are missing, and the OroEo and OroAt."

They then sat down and talked about kin they shared in common. The women from the house appeared and the recently arrived men asked them to roast fish. The women also offered them Brazil nuts. They ate, since they were very hungry, and said that they had been afraid of the Wari' arrows. An OroMon man said that these new Whites had arrived just after they had roasted and eaten his older sister, who had been killed by a White man from the region. With these other Whites, newly arrived from afar, things were different, they said, since they treated them as though they were their people—that is, they made the Wari' their kin, as though the Wari' were their children.

Paletó's father-in-law, Jamain To'u, continued to test the new arrivals to confirm they really were Wari'. Speaking the same language was not enough. After all, with short-cropped hair and wearing clothes, accompanied by White people, they certainly resembled enemies. He asked if they knew how to sing *tamara*, one kind of Wari' music. They proudly replied: "We haven't got a bad throat!" Paletó then sang for me the music that they had sung there, vivid still in his memory. Afterwards the house residents had sung as well, and everyone went off to sleep.

The next day, those who had arrived invited them to go where the Whites were. "Let's go to see the real Whites! Be brave! They call us their people." They went to where the Whites were waiting and met the Kanoê man called Saul.

He carried a 22-caliber rifle, which, according to Paletó, he would have used to kill the Wari' if needed. The OroNao' from the other shore, who already had known the Whites for some time, explained to them that the rifle would not kill them and that they need not be afraid. Saul shot a capuchin monkey and the Wari' ran off, startled. After all, Paletó said, they knew the sound of gunshots only too well. They returned, killed birds and monkeys, and ate.

When they arrived in Koxain, they were astonished. It was all cleared, weeded, with no undergrowth. Then they saw the Whites. Fernando Cruz, Father Roberto, and Rui wore glasses. All the Whites wore glasses. "We were scared," Paletó said, "and we shrank back." Fernando Cruz laughed loudly. "Come, come," he said, according to the OroNao' of the other shore, who worked as a translator since he already knew a little of the White men's language. They seemed happy, patting the Wari' on the arms and offering them axes. After a few days, the wives of the OroNao' appeared, who had come with the Whites and until then had been at the Barracão Velho encampment downriver. They helped the recently contacted Wari' by cooking for them. Some of the women, whom I met on the Negro River, would later marry the Wari' from there. "Don't be afraid of me," said one of the women, Kimoi, provocatively, "I don't have a husband." She pointed to one of the young men from there, laughing, "You're going to be my husband!" "I already have a wife," he replied. "If she dies, I'll marry you," Kimoi retorted.

13.
SEXY

IMAGINE THE SCENE: the women enticing the men, as they used to do by plucking out the men's wooden earrings, licking them and hurling them on the ground, as an invitation for sex. Paletó used to tell me that some of the women—those who were born with ambiguous genitalia—would joke provocatively to embarrass the men. When the male guests arrived for a festival, many of them young men, an intersex woman would invite one of the men to sit on her lap. Naked, she would then rub her genitals against the man's buttocks. Prevented by the rules of good manners from standing up, he would remain sitting there, increasingly flustered. At the awkward sight, the women would laugh a lot. When, after contact, the Whites learned of Wari' intersex people, they decided to take these babies to Guajará for surgery. Not surprisingly, they died, and the mothers began to hide these children from the Whites, clothing them all the time. Still today, they remain clothed even when bathing, and try to conceal their androgynous features with large shirts and a constant silence to hide their masculine voices. Before the Whites arrived in the region, these women would marry and adopt their sisters' children as their own. Today they stay single, clothed, and desexualized.

I took a trip to the city of Ji-Paraná, in Rondônia, with Abrão and Paletó. There, Abrão composed a three-page text for me about our experience, written in the Wari' language. I encountered it again when I revisited my notebooks:

> My father and I left for Ji-Paraná. My father was happy to meet other White people. Early in the morning, we drank coffee; at ten o'clock, we drank fruit juice; at twelve o'clock, we ate rice, beans, chicken and leaves. In the afternoon, we ate again. At night, we watched TV.

The most interesting detail is found on the last page of the text, where Abrão recounts that, after waking early and taking a shower, his father said that he had dreamed of having sex with a White woman, who had invited him: "Come and have sex with me, come and have sex with me!" "So," Abrão continues, "we went to tell this dream to my older sister [me] and she laughed a lot!" Speaking freely about sex is typical of the Wari' and, judging by what my anthropologist colleagues recount, of many other Indigenous peoples too. Paletó, during the times he was in Rio de Janeiro, frequently told us his dreams, and many of them involved sex, mostly with his wife To'o, who had stayed back in the village, but also with other Wari' women. We laughed together a lot, especially when the accounts involved strange women.

One particularly memorable episode occurred on the first trip Paletó and Abrão made to Rio de Janeiro, in December 1992. At that time, video rental shops still existed (and VHS!) and we would visit one close to our house, where we chose a diverse range of movies together, among them *Quest for Fire*, the 1981 French-Canadian fantasy film about Paleolithic Europe, and another on cannibalism in New Guinea, the name of which I have forgotten but which I recall they enjoyed greatly. The colorful covers of the videos were displayed on the shelves, arranged by genre. On one visit, Paletó's attention was drawn, even before Abrão's, to the area where photos of naked women could be seen. It was the porn movie section, which, before the advent of the internet, was practically the only source available for these types of films. I tried to distract him, but Paletó began to take the video boxes off the shelf, one by one, and ask me to read the synopses of the films on the back covers. Ashamed—after all, he was a father to me—I began to read, until one of them particularly caught his interest. It was a parody of *Back to the Future*, then a recent hit. We rented the film at the insistence of Paletó, who asked to see it when we got back home. I had to be present to translate, he said, though he soon discovered there was virtually no dialogue in the film. But the plot—what plot there was at all—still had to be translated. As in the original film, the protagonist returns to the past and meets his parents when they were young. In the porn version, though, he has sex with his mother, a tremendously sexy young woman, in a scene that takes up a fair amount of the film's running time. Embarrassed to watch these scenes of explicit sex with my father, worse still incestuous sex, I also had to answer his many questions. He asked me whether these women were not ashamed to show their anus, which he called the "maize cake path." Watching the women moan and scream at the moment of orgasm, he asked me whether they were going to die. Eventually, he declared that he was sorry for all of them because they did not know how to have sex properly. I told him about women who dance naked in strip clubs, and when I explained to him that this is their job, he replied, "But don't they write on paper, like you?" Fortunately, he had no desire to repeat the experience on future trips, the video rental shops all closed, and, as far as I know, ready access to the internet on visits to Guajará-Mirim means that the Wari', especially the young men, have ample access to (and a keen interest in) porn films.

Certainly, the unusualness of the sex in the porn version of *Back to the Future* was much more my impression than theirs. Wari' myths, considered to be events that happened in the distant past, and told in a family setting, generally from grandfathers or fathers to sons and daughters, are full of sex scenes, whether between people or with animals pretending to be people. In the myth of the vulture people, for example, which Paletó told me more than once, a man ejaculates inside a woman, even though she had advised him not to do so. As punishment, his penis grows so long that he has to walk around with it rolled up in a little basket hanging from his shoulder. When he wants to have sex, he places his penis on the ground and it slithers along the paths until nestling between the legs of a random woman, who is startled but does not refuse. In another myth, an old woman is killed and dismembered. Only her clitoris remains, which hides in various places to provoke her killers with jokes and laughter. I was surprised when an adult man chose this myth to tell in the middle of a Christmas mass, celebrated by emeritus bishop Dom Roberto in Sagarana village. Soon after the Gospel reading, which spoke of the three wise men and baby Jesus, the bishop asked for some of the Wari' present (the mass was for them) to tell a story of the ancestors that had some relation to the Gospel. The man went up to the altar and began to speak in Wari', in a low voice, as they usually do. I could hardly believe my ears when I realized which myth he had chosen. To the Wari' present, the choice did not seem in the least bit odd. The bishop, blessed by not understanding the Wari' language well, did not know what it was about, wore a smile on his face throughout the entire narrative, and, at the end, thanked the man.

As well as their free imagination and verbal expression of thoughts about sex, I was also delighted by the way in which the Wari' treated their own body and the bodies of others. One time, during my first months, as I approached Paletó's house, I saw him lying down and completely naked, with his daughters picking ticks from his thighs. On seeing me, they immediately stopped. Paletó entered the house and put on some shorts. At the end of his life, though, he was no longer ashamed in front of me, and more than once I lowered his trousers so he could pee. In 2005, when I was living with Paletó and To'o in Sagarana, I wrote in my field diary: "I like this way of the Wari', this way of everything with the body being public: they fart, burp, pick their nose. Today, when To'o arrived at Luisa's house, she laughed, spoke two words, and began to pick nits from her."

Picking nits is a form of conversation, and permission is never asked: someone else's head is always freely accessible. At first, I suffered from a lack of nits, because as soon as someone began to mess with my hair, they lost interest. One day I was surprised by the interest of a woman who had finally found a nit on me and I became a legitimate participant in this mute conversation via the body. I have two beautiful photos of my sons. In one of them, Francisco, fourteen years old, wearing a blue T-shirt and long trousers, is lying with his head on a big sack full of Brazil nuts, on a stilt palm platform, with a closed book in his hands. Around his head are his grandmother To'o, his aunt Ja, and a young girl, searching attentively in his hair for nits. His eyes are half-closed. In the other photo is André, around five years old, dressed in a brightly colored striped shirt and red trousers. His head lays on the lap of a young woman, sitting on a stilt palm platform, searching through his hair. In his mouth is a large yellow starfruit, clutched in his hands.

These memories suddenly transport me to a completely different context, many years later, when I realized that access to the head of others, unmediated by words, was in fact a delightful peculiarity of the Wari'. I was in a massage parlor

in Siem Riep, Cambodia, a place called Lemon Grass, where they served us tea made from the same herb while we waited. The people of the country, especially the inhabitants of the mountains with their physical features and their thatched houses, reminded me of the Wari' and from time to time I found myself thinking about the latter, and in words from their own language, as if I could make myself understood using them there. Already addicted to foot massages, I decided to have a body massage, which was going marvelously just like the others, when I was surprised by the question, in English: "Can I touch your head?" Yes, please.

14.
TALKING WITH THE BISHOP AND THE MISUNDERSTANDINGS OF CONTACT

I N MARCH 1995, I was invited by members of the Indigenist Missionary Council to present a seminar for them on the Wari' relationship to Christianity. This was a topic I had begun to study and indeed wished to discuss with the religious and lay missionaries. The seminar would be held in the city of Ji-Paraná, Rondônia. I decided to swap the cash payment they offered me for the right to take two guests, Paletó and Abrão, whom I went to fetch on the Negro River. We made the five-hour journey from Guajará-Mirim to Ji-Paraná in a pickup truck. On arrival, we were lodged in a large house, located a short distance from the city, with many rooms, a spacious refectory, and an ample conference room where the classes would be held. They put me in a room next to Paletó and Abrão, meaning that we had a week of intense conviviality, especially during the many meals and snacks. They were delighted by the surfeit of food. The text written by Abrão about this trip ends with his perception of Paletó's importance to me: "Only our father helps us by knowing the stories of the ancestors. That's why my older sister knows. If my father didn't exist, she wouldn't know."

As well as various missionaries, the Catholic priest Roberto Arruda was also present at the seminar, now holding the title of bishop (emeritus, since he had retired). He had participated in the first contacts. A tall, strong man, gray-haired and firm-voiced, in his seventies, he still spoke with an accent typical of the interior of São Paulo state. He admired the Wari' greatly, and after his retirement began to spend much of his time in Sagarana village, where he would eventually die and be buried. The Wari' referred to him as "our grandfather." One day after dinner, still sitting at the long table, I asked him for a detailed account of the contact expedition in which he had participated, so I could record him. Sitting next to me was Paletó, who had been present in the events narrated by Dom Roberto, though they did not speak the same language, neither during the first encounter nor then in Ji-Paraná. I acted as a translator, summarizing blocks of Dom Roberto's narrative for Paletó, who then was keen to recount what had happened from his perspective, which I sought to translate back to Dom Roberto. What became abundantly clear were the misunderstandings generated in the encounter, which, thirty years later, even appeared amusing.

Among other things, Dom Roberto told us that he only learned about the episode of the attack on the White man in the canoe, Joaquim, when he returned to the camp they had set up a little farther downriver. He had spent the entire day walking around the area, searching for the best places to leave presents for the Indigenous people, even visiting Koxain. The episode occurred on June 26, 1961, a month after the expedition's departure from Guajará-Mirim. Back at the camp, they told him that when Joaquim was hit, Xijan, who was also in the canoe, stood up and began to speak to the warriors in Wari'. Not knowing what was going on, the Whites who were in the camp, hearing the noise from afar, grabbed their rifles in the expectation that they were going to hunt peccaries. However, the Wari', realizing what was happening, removed their clothes and got into the water to follow the warriors, shouting things that the Whites did not understand. One of them was exactly the man who ended up encountering Jimon Pan Tokwe on the path to Koxain, talked to him, and walked with him to his house in Terem Matam. They probably narrowly missed Dom Roberto since he had just departed from Koxain, where he had left, he said, a small aluminum cauldron and a machete.

According to Dom Roberto, there were around six houses in Koxain, three of them burned to the ground, probably in an arson attack by Whites, he concluded. As the Wari' never mentioned an attack there, I imagine that the houses had been burned by them following a sickness or death. The three remaining houses were in good shape and one of them had an enormous pile of maize, as was the custom among the Wari'. That was undoubtedly where Jimon had been heading when he was encountered.

When the Whites went to Koxain to wait for the people arriving from Terem Matam, already accompanied by various Wari' who were in the encampment, Paletó met Dom Roberto and noted his glasses and those of the other men, which he described as strange eyes. Paletó says that they all sat on the platforms of the houses, but in Dom Roberto's recollection, they sat on mats around a fire. Conversation was difficult, Dom Roberto said, because Antônio Costa—the man who already knew the OroNao' of the other shore, a territorial group who had lived with the Whites for five years, and who served as an interpreter, forming a pair with a Wari' man called Wem Kanum—understood almost nothing of what the new Wari' were saying.

In the series of misperceptions that ensued, Dom Roberto, through the two interpreters, asked them to identify the chiefs of the Wari', unaware that they have no chiefs or any notion of hierarchy. That was when three men approached: Paletó, his father-in-law Jamain To'u, and Wem Tawinain. They offered bows and arrows to the Whites, which, for Dom Roberto, was a sign of peace, and for Paletó, the giving of a gift. There, in the refectory in Ji-Paraná, Dom Roberto was surprised to learn that Paletó was one of the men who first stood before them. I thought to myself, who else could it have been but Paletó, with his curiosity always bubbling to the surface, ready to be engaged.

I have photos of the exact moment, which I obtained in the archives of the Guajará Prelacy. The photos date back fifty-six years, meaning that Paletó must have been around thirty years old. He had already lost his father, a wife, and a daughter, all killed, and was now living with To'o and their small daughter, Orowao Karaxu. At the left of one of the photos is Fernando Cruz, wearing his glasses, dressed in 1950s style with trousers, belt, and short-sleeved shirt, buttoned up and tucked into his trousers, and with very short hair, resembling a military cut. He is being handed a bow and some arrows by Jamain To'u who, naked, is already wearing a fake necklace. Next to him, facing the photographer, is Paletó, his hair cut in the traditional style for men, ear-length with a center parting, gazing very attentively and also holding a bow and arrows. Next to him, partially covered by

Fernando Cruz, is another man, probably Wem Tawinain, also with his weapons ready to be offered. In another photo, the same men are now standing next to then Father Roberto, who is wearing glasses and a white full-length cassock, and another White man, younger, whom we were unable to identify. In this photo, Father Roberto is smiling, looking up at Paletó and Jamain To'u as they aim their bows skywards. Paletó, with his face partially covered by the arm pulling the bowstring, is laughing.

Probably because the Whites took Jamain To'u to be a chief, they gave him the fake necklace, which he certainly wore to be polite. The same must have happened too with various other men, who appear in another photo in a line, with the forest as a backdrop, naked and wearing necklaces. And not just the necklaces. According to Dom Roberto, they gave the "chief" Jamain To'u most of the metal tools that they had brought as gifts, for him to hand out to his people. According to Paletó, Jamain To'u, not a chief at all, had just been lucky: he was carrying a basket, which meant he was able to take a much larger quantity of tools than the others.

While Paletó's interventions at the conversation dwelt on the names of the people present, on the strange appearance of the Whites, and on the quantity of food they received, Dom Roberto spoke about the disastrous preparations for

the expedition. He recalled that, on leaving, they had estimated a population of three hundred Wari' when calculating the amount of medications to take, but encountered around three thousand. In the first few days, men from the Indian Protection Service (SPI) appeared, among them the well-known *sertanista* Francisco Meireles, and soon afterward, the epidemics began, which Dom Roberto attributed to this visit, even though admitting that no examination had been made of the Whites or of the Indigenous people who participated in their own expedition. The one who met Jimon Pan Tokwe on the path to Koxain and chatted with him, called Orowao Powa, contacted a month earlier, was weak and sick, and soon had to return.

As soon as he saw the sicknesses begin, Dom Roberto traveled downriver by motorboat to Guajará-Mirim with the aim of obtaining medicines and taking them back to the Wari'. It was the end of June 1961. Without any credit, they were unable to obtain anything in the city. Only later, after many difficulties, did they receive boxes of medicines sent from São Paulo by the bishop Dom Rey, who had traveled there for that purpose. When they were getting ready to travel upriver again to the Wari', Fernando Cruz, who was in Brasília, asked for them to wait for him. According to Dom Roberto, on arriving in Guajará, Fernando Cruz headed straight for the annual festival of the neighboring Bolivian city, Guayaramerín, on August 6. He only reappeared on August 8, drunk, to embark in Guajará. With so much time passed, the diseases had already spread. It was this same Fernando Cruz who, according to Dom Roberto, decided to take a group of people, Wari' men and women, to the rubber plantations of the upper Pacaás Novos River, soon after contact, so that, by proving their pacification to the rubber tappers, he could enjoy the beer festival promised by the rubber boss Manoel Lucindo, one of the main figures responsible for ordering the massacres of the Wari'.

Paletó was also in this group. Telling me about this event many years after our trip to Ji-Paraná, he recalled that as they traveled upriver, Fernando Cruz would explain to the rubber tappers whom they met on the way—clearly afraid of the Wari'—that the latter were now his people and that they would no longer attack them. The wives of the rubber tappers hid out of fear, but Fernando Cruz said that they should not be afraid. In a festive atmosphere, he asked the Wari' to paint the rubber tappers and their wives with annatto. Some Wari' men stayed in the rubber plantations there, working for the Whites, and only joined their kin years later. One of them was Awo Kamip, Paletó's nephew. Having learned Portuguese with the rubber tappers, he later served as an interpreter for the missionaries on the Negro River, which led him to become a pastor.

This, though, was not the first incursion of the priests into Wari' territory. In November 1950, a Benedictine priest, Mauro Wirth, ignoring the advice of Bishop Dom Rey, journeyed up the Ouro Preto, an affluent of the right shore of the Pacaás Novos, accompanied part of the way by woodsmen, in search of the already famous "wild Indians," disposed, in the words of the local newspaper, to "gather them into the flock of the Lord." After this point, no more was heard of him for a year, until an expedition left in search of him and found pieces of his cassock, together with the various presents he had taken for the Wari', untouched inside a black leather suitcase. The Wari' perfectly recalled the priest, who, according to them, did not think straight. They said that he wore long clothing and glasses, sat alone in an empty Wari' house, and began to shout out, calling them, before starting to play a harmonica. They watched him for a while and decided to shoot him. "We thought he would take our women," one man told me.

15.
THE EPIDEMICS

THE EPIDEMICS OF FLU, pneumonia, and diarrhea that
followed the first contacts on the Negro River were a huge
catastrophe, which, combined with the massacres that preceded contact, decimated about two-thirds of the Wari' population, especially affecting those who fled from the Whites and
did not receive medicines and injections right from the start.

Paletó recounted that the day after the first encounter they already started coughing and, one by one, were
forced to lie down on the house platforms. They were sick.
"The Whites are bad, we said!" Then an OroNao' man
arrived from the group contacted five years previously,
who said to them: "Come quickly, the Whites will give
you injections!" All of them went—men, their wives, and
their children. On the way, some people who had already
become extremely sick had to be carried. They wanted to
carry Paletó since he was coughing heavily, but he preferred to continue walking. At that moment, he said, some
people were very angry with the Whites, remembering the
many relatives killed by them. They walked and walked
and finally arrived at another camp of the Whites. A man
called Antônio Costa was there, an SPI employee, the one

named as an occasional translator between the Wari' and the Whites in Dom Roberto's account. He brought the syringes and needles in his hands. On catching sight of them, the Wari' pulled away. "We don't want them, we don't want those thorns," they said. Finally, one of the OroNao', Wem Kanum, held out his arm to show the new arrivals that they would not die from the White man's thorn. "Ah, okay," the others said after seeing him receiving the injection. Paletó and the others who were coughing were given medicated syrup. Medications and treatment were given throughout the night.

One man, Maxun Taparape, decided not to follow the group and, leaving Koxain, traveled upriver to the land of the OroEo and OroAt, to tell them about the arrival of the Whites and all that was happening. There were many Oro-Nao' there too, his kin, fleeing from the Whites as Paletó had done before. Maxun Taparape decided to make a joke that went awry. When they saw him arrive, they said: "Our grandfather has arrived!" Waving a machete, he responded: "We've turned into Whites, we've turned into Whites!" "Let's run!" the Wari' exclaimed to their wives. "It must be the ghost of the White man we killed some time ago!" Many fled to the forest. Others, doubtful, insisted that it was their grandfather. Finally, realizing his antics had been poorly timed, he explained that the Whites were calling them. They went with him to Koxain to fetch tools, but, still suspicious, returned to their lands afterward. And they began to die, on the path, in the houses, in the forest. "Few OroEo survived," Paletó concluded, "and all the fault of crazy Maxun Taparape, who didn't know how to explain properly, who joked around when he should have spoken seriously."

All of the Wari' remember the sound of people coughing and moaning, and the sight of people becoming extremely thin, since they had not planted crops and were too weak to hunt. They walked from one location to another, trying to escape the disease, and died on the trails. Orowao Kun, Paletó's son-in-law, said to me that, then a young man, he carried his mother some of the way, but she died and he had to abandon her to the vultures, which filled him with horror. They could not eat their dead, or even burn them, since the survivors were also too thin and weak. To'o, Paletó's wife, became gravely ill and almost died. "I don't know how we survived," Paletó said. He himself became slightly sick and soon recovered (he "didn't know how to die") and was part of the group of men who went to the land of the OroEo, in the region of Kit, the source of the stone axes, to try to give them medications.

Dom Roberto spoke of many men going on this expedition to the OroEo, himself included. On the way they stopped at Hwijimain Xitot, where Paletó had once lived, and twenty sick people received injections. Paletó tells that when they arrived close to Kit, everyone removed their clothes, save for the priest, Fernando Cruz, Rui, and another assistant called Assis. Even José Grande, the cook, removed his clothes. On the path they saw the corpses. They arrived at the port of the OroEo and found them very thin: "The OroEo no longer had bodies!" When they saw Antônio Costa prepare the syringe to give injections, they reacted in the same way as the others had earlier: "We don't want this thorn, we're afraid of the thorn!" This time it was Hwerein Pe e', Paletó's nephew, who offered his arm for the injection to show them not to be afraid.

Dom Roberto recalled that many of the houses in Kit were burned down (presumably due to the deaths) and that there was very little water, which he boiled to give to the sick. The latter were then carried to Kit by other Wari', where they were treated. There was much diarrhea, coughing, and fever, he recalled. They spent the whole night listening to people groan. Hwerein Pe e' asked the priest to give them something for the pain, and Dom Roberto had the idea of giving massages with camphor. He remembered one woman who had been very sick, and Paletó immediately added (on hearing my version for him) that it was the mother of A'ain Xit, currently a resident of the Negro River, who got better with the camphor. Paletó imitated her panting and wheezing as she tried to breathe.

On our trip to Kit in 2002, we found, precisely in the place where we camped close to the river, old medicine vials, the kind made from thick blue glass, scattered over the ground. It seems nobody had returned there in these forty years separating the two voyages. When we looked at the glass bottles without understanding what they were doing there, the OroEo men quickly identified them as medicine vials, and the spot as the place where they had medicated the sick. According to Dom Roberto, the rapid response to streptomycin was not enough to assuage this episode of death en masse.

I am unable to grasp the scale of the horror experienced by the Wari', even with the help of photos of extremely thin people, similar to those we have seen in the famous images from Biafra, Nigeria, at the end of the 1960s, or Ethiopia in the 1970s. Some of the most shocking I have seen show the terminal illness and death of a child, who was then cut up and deposited on a funeral grill. Not only was the child skeletal but also the people weeping for her, clutching her in their arms. Taken by a reporter from the magazine *O Cruzeiro (The Cruise)*, sent to the site to verify the existence of cannibalism, the publication of the photos was vetoed by a group of eminent anthropologists in an attempt to avoid any prejudiced action by local inhabitants against the already debilitated Indigenous population. Kept by someone unknown, they surprisingly ended up in my hands in December 1987, when, giving a lecture on Wari' funerary cannibalism in Belém, I was approached by a photographer who offered me the photos as a gift. Amazed, back in Rio de Janeiro I received, via a carrier, a series of negatives, which I developed myself in my home studio in Santa Teresa. I passed sleepless nights, not because of the idea of cannibalism they contained, but because of the image of those faces of pure bone, with enormous, bulging eyes, and curved bodies, almost skeletons, that emerged there in my home, under the red light in the developing bath.

16.
GUAJARÁ-MIRIM, BRAZIL

"WE'LL SINK, we'll sink!" Paletó thought to himself as he boarded a large boat for the first time. After the visit to the rubber plantations, a group of Wari' men, led by Fernando Cruz, traveled down the entire Pacaás Novos to its confluence with the Mamoré, arriving eventually at Guajará-Mirim. It was the start of October, Dom Roberto recalled. Fernando Cruz wanted to show the Wari' to the White people of the city and receive plaudits for his feat. As Dom Roberto had stayed behind to care for the sick at the Barracão camp on the Negro River, Fernando Cruz was left to deal with the bishop, Dom Rey, when they reached Guajará, and to explain the whereabouts of their priest. Gilberto Gama, the other man from the SPI, traveled downriver with them, but fell out with the bishop over rumors of his sexual relations with Indigenous women. The police were forced to intervene, and Gilberto was dispatched outside the region.

Paletó said that they spent many days in Guajará. As soon as they arrived, they were bought clothes so that they could meet the Whites. "We didn't have clothes, and they only looked at our penises!" The Whites asked them to show

how to use a bow and arrow, and the Wari' demonstrated by shooting at trees. Fernando then took them to the barracks. Paletó laughs as he remembers how they had no idea what bread was. When they saw it spread with butter, they thought the bread was rotten and refused to eat it.

How can we imagine this first sight of a city by people who had never left the forest? Not that Guajará-Mirim was a large city in 1961. Nor is it today, with around 47,000 inhabitants. At that time, the city, today sprawling with many outlying neighborhoods, was concentrated on the shores of the Mamoré, where houses can still be seen that were built facing the port in the 1920s, when the settlement acquired city status. One of these houses on the river shore, built a bit later, was, until recently, the head office of the local Funai. In front of a square, with a bandstand in the middle, is the city's diocese, called the prelacy at that time, where the bishop Dom Rey and the priest Roberto lived, and which Paletó and his companions visited on that voyage. The barracks, also mentioned by Paletó, are located farther from this center.

Visible along the river shore are remnants of the famous Madeira-Mamoré Railway. Inaugurated in 1912, it was deactivated in 1972 and much of the track that led to Porto Velho was covered by the asphalt of the highway connecting the two cities. Whenever I make this trip by coach, rattled by the numerous holes in the road, it pains me to see those sections of track still showing through the blacktop, as well as the narrow iron bridges built for the passage of the train, which cost so many lives to construct. In the 1980s, on my first trips, part of the road was still dirt, and when it rained, some sections became so flooded that the outbound coach had to wait for the returning coach so that the passengers could transfer by foot from one to the other, hauling their luggage with them through the mud. Each coach then turned around and went back the way it had come. The old train station became the city museum, with two old locomotives on display outside.

Construction of the railway affected the life of the Wari', since some of its sections passed close to the territory of the OroWaram territorial group, at the mouth of the Laje River, which flows into the Madeira. The train brought more people to the region, especially rubber tappers, who then entered Wari' lands and killed them. According to what Dom Roberto told me, the Wari' ended up destroying some of the infrastructure, and for this reason some of the rail tracks were electrified. Although I never heard of Wari' entering the city before the first peaceful contacts, I know of various episodes of expeditions to shoot arrows at the train itself on

its journey, a strange body from which Whites emerged. The latter were also shot. One of my Wari' friends, now deceased, received the name of Delegado after he shot the *delegado* (police chief) of Guajará-Mirim who had been cycling alongside the track.

It is not difficult to imagine the tense atmosphere of this period and the animosity of the local inhabitants toward the Wari', expressed perfectly in a report from the local newspaper, *O Imparcial (The Impartial)*, dated January 8, 1961—thus before contact with either the OroWaram and their neighbors, or the Wari' of the Negro River:

> Recently—for around the last two months—it seems that the Indians of this region have suffered some kind of a hydrophobic trance. They are emboldened and attack with an unabashed audacity. This behavior seems strange to us . . . considering that the savage is instinctively cautious and fearful of the "Whites." Their bloodthirsty nature is that of the trapped tiger who attacks for no reason, driven only by the natural desire to defend itself, which constitutes the egocentric system, a sublime force transmitted to the animal instinct in order to conserve the breath of life. They are humans, albeit products of a different field and we consider them a kind of hybrid creation.

In the same newspaper, some days earlier, on January 1, 1961, the following appeared:

> Action is needed and a lot of it. Tearful interviews will not give life or health to those who labor in our forests, in search of resources for our survival. They need to be

protected from this horde of cold-blooded killers who infest the forests, protected by absurd laws that deprive regions like this one from effective development.

Although Paletó lived far from there and took no part in these expeditions to the train line and the outskirts of Guajará, he was taken to the latter city to reassure the Whites that now "they were well behaved." After these days in the city, Paletó's group again boarded a large boat, which traveled upriver toward the upper Negro, where the SPI base Barracão Velho was located. The sick people being treated were still there, along with all the others. It had been some time since they had seen their wives, Paletó observed, because only men had gone on this trip to Guajará. "Your mother was there," he said to me, referring to his wife To'o. She was completely cured. They went to plant crops in Mana Arup. The priest then disappeared, Paletó said referring to Dom Roberto, "We saw no more of the priests' people!" Dom Roberto, sitting next to him at the table, added that it was the director of the SPI who had said that he did not want to see the priest's face there again. However, he still kept going to regions closer to the city whenever he was called to treat sick people.

On the journey back upriver, some Wari' stayed behind in Tanajura, located on the left shore of the Pacaás Novos, inhabited by the Wari' who had been isolated for years and had been contacted, some five years earlier, by the Evangelical missionaries. Wan e', my first father, was one of those who stayed. He was later joined by my mother, Orowao Xik Waje and two of their children, Jamain and Maxun Hat (the one who broke his rib playing soccer and said he was going to die). They were boys still and, like the others, were quickly catechized by the Evangelical missionaries living there. Paletó once told me that the people of the Negro River only truly converted after they were visited by Jamain and Maxun Hat, by then young men, when they spoke to them about the God presented by the missionaries. "How is it that you all became believers?" I asked. "From Jamain and Maxun Hat," Paletó promptly replied.

17.
MEETING THE MISSIONARIES

IT WAS SOME MONTHS after the first contact, after the
voyage to the city and back again to Koxain, that the Wari'
of the Negro River region were to meet Royal Taylor, a Ca-
nadian missionary from the New Tribes Mission. He col-
laborated with the team of missionaries who had made the
first contact with the Wari', those on the other shore of the
Pacaás Novos, and with the Wari' of the Laje River region,
one month before the contact made on the Negro River by
the Catholic priests. Learning about the contact there, and the
absence of the priest and his team, who had gone to the city,
the Protestant missionaries immediately settled among them.

Royal, who was an old man when we met in 1994, was
still young, with a strong body, Paletó said. As he already
knew something of the Wari' language, he immediately began
to preach to the new arrivals in Koxain: "God is good, He
is the one who created the Wari'." At night, everyone gathered under what Paletó described as a large mosquito net
while Royal preached. "His wife, Joanna, wrote down our
language," Paletó said. Royal said:

God created the toads, He created the ducks, He created

all the animals, all the fish, the water, the rain, the sun, the moon, the stars, the clouds, He created us too, and our grandfather Adam. That's why we exist. He also created all the Whites. I came from very far away, God told me to come, to not let them kill you, my brothers and sisters.

Paletó says that the Wari' found this talk about the creation of things very strange, and that they looked at each other questioningly, asking each other: what is all this about? "Some just listened, others laughed. He sang a song like this: 'Let's rise on high, let's rise on high, the true high of God.'" Royal also told them that Jesus came, people did not like him, they killed him, and he came back to life.

A Wari' woman, Kimoi, thought that was very strange: "The White man is saying that he died and came back to life!" "So that's why he limps!" they concluded. He was a dead person! The news spread. The misunderstanding was soon cleared up by a man who had been taken to Manaus by Royal and received Christian teachings. "It was Jesus who rose from the dead, not Royal," he explained. Listening to all of this, Paletó said he remained silent. For a long time he did not want to be a believer.

According to Paletó's recollections, Royal went to Guajará. In his place, and already at Barracão Velho, the SPI base, arrived Leroy, another American, who continued Royal's preaching. The Wari' continued not to understand what it was all about. "I don't know, I don't know," they would say. Leroy's first wife and daughter had died in an airplane accident and he had since remarried. The missionary Barbara Kern also already lived in the region, Paletó recalled. Barbara was very young, and not too long after she arrived she married a missionary colleague from Germany. The two lived for around thirty years among the Wari' almost without interruption.

Barbara was one of the main translators of the Bible into the Wari' language. I met her and her husband on my first trip, in 1986, and was delighted by her kindness. When our boat broke down one time close to Tanajura, as we were heading upriver from Guajará to Santo André, Barbara put up Beth and me in her house. She even offered us cookies at breakfast, something impossible to forget when one is in the forest. Years later, when I spent some time in Tanajura with Francisco while he was very young, he became very sick. I ran fifteen minutes along the trail connecting the village to Barbara's house, carrying Francisco, then a year old, on my back, feverish and sluggish. There was not a single boat at the Funai post where we lived and I knew that I had to take him to the city as quickly as possible. I arrived at Barbara's house gasping for breath and immediately started weeping desperately. She gently calmed me with a cup of water mixed with sugar. In less than half an hour they prepared the boat to take us to Guajará. There it was determined that Francisco had a severe urinary infection, successfully treated with antibiotics. Although I cannot accept their imposition of Christian ideas upon the Wari', which in my view undermines what is most vital in Wari' culture, I shall always be grateful for the help they gave me at that moment. With them, and with other friends that I made in Guajará, I learned that solidarity in these remote regions can overcome ideological divergences.

In recalling those early times, Paletó spoke at length about Barbara, saying that she had given birth to her children while in the village. He was surprised years later to see that

Paletó talking with me through Skype

her firstborn, Jonathan, whom Paletó knew as a baby, already
had white hair. Paletó always liked Barbara. I reconnected
them via Skype in my home, he in Rio and she in Germany,
for a conversation those many years later.

18.

IN THE LAND OF THE PRIESTS

A FTER LIVING for about four years at Barracão Velho, the SPI base on the upper Negro River, in the company of Royal and other Protestant missionaries, Paletó and his family were invited to move to Sagarana, an agricultural colony founded by the Prelacy of Guajará-Mirim in 1965. It was already inhabited by various Wari' from the OroMon, Oro-Waram, and OroWaramXijein territorial groups, as well as people from other Indigenous groups, like the Makurap and Kanoê. Sagarana was located entirely outside the traditional Wari' territory, at the confluence of the Mamoré and Guaporé Rivers, and had been given to the priests by a Catholic institution for them to shelter sick people who arrived at the city hospital from the villages.

Construction of the Sagarana base was initially supervised by the priest Roberto Arruda, but due to the bishop Dom Rey's sickness, the former had to take over the prelacy in 1965 and was appointed bishop the following year. Administration of Sagarana was then passed to a Lithuanian man, Bendoraites, who claimed to be a priest and doctor and was active in the treatment of the Wari' who arrived sick in the city. In Sagarana they had rigid work hours, were forced to obey hygiene rules, and were banned from holding festivals or singing their own music.

"Father" Bendoraites visited Sagarana sporadically, leaving day-to-day care of the colony in the hands of a young Bolivian man named Antenor, who used violent techniques to achieve his objectives. The Wari' told me that he threatened the Indigenous population with guns, constructed a jail with a door and padlock to imprison those who committed infractions like stealing chickens, and chained those women who practiced abortion. Talking to me about this, one man remembered a wife and children crying for the father, who was imprisoned in the underground jail, communicating with him through the funeral song. From within the locked hole, the prisoner told his family, also through the funeral song, that he was going to die. Some tried to escape, but they were pursued by Antenor and ended up returning, in part because their unfamiliarity with the territory meant that they could not find their way. In short, a sixteenth-century mission in the heart of the twentieth century. Unsurprisingly, therefore, those people who lived there at the time rejected the prelacy's version that the place was intended for health treatment; rather, they concluded that they had been taken there as a punishment. It was a prison from which escape seemed impossible.

There was practically no religious instruction at the mission. Antenor and Bendoraites did not speak the Wari' language, but masses were held, which Paletó describes as follows:

> They gave us a piece of maize cake [wafer] which vanished when we put it in our mouths. There was also a really alcoholic drink [for the priest], many oil lamps

were lit, and they knelt. We sat down too and sang in Sagarana. I didn't understand the name of the music. We just sang with our eyes closed. Afterwards, Amen.

Bendoraites, it was later discovered, was not a doctor or a priest, and took advantage of his visits to Sagarana to act out his homosexual fantasies, offering presents to the men for them to masturbate him. Talking to some of these men one time, in Paletó's company, I was surprised to learn that they found this funny, a ridiculous behavior on the part of the priest, which in some ways was beneficial to them, since they just had to "work on the priest's cock" to obtain coveted goods like hammocks and blankets. Bendoraites also took photos of the Wari' women naked to send to Europe, he said, in exchange for donations. All of this occurred out of the sight and knowledge of the bishop and other priests, who rarely visited Sagarana and unsurprisingly were not kept informed by him as to the details of what happened there. Dom Geraldo Verdier, the bishop who succeeded Dom Roberto, and who died some months after Paletó, was horrified when I told him, using all the euphemisms I could dream up, about the sexual adventures of the fake priest. At that moment, the latter was imprisoned in a jail in the neighboring Bolivian city, Guayaramerín, accused of killing a young man, his lover. Recently, I read in a newspaper that an important politician from Lithuania had discovered that one of its citizens had lived in Rondônia and had been a true hero. The newspaper stated that a filmmaker was preparing to film his life. I imagine the surprise the Lithuanians will have when they arrive in Brazil.

Paletó tells that the "priest's people" convinced him to go to Sagarana, claiming that they needed him to teach the others how to work. Knowing Paletó, I imagine that he was exceedingly curious to see this new location. Moreover, kin of his wife To'o, from the OroMon territorial group, were already living there. Among them was Toji, To'o's uncle, the younger brother of her father Jamain To'u, who had died of sickness at Barracão. As was common then, Toji had married one of his brother's widows, To'o's mother's sister. Paletó was going to live among his in-laws, but also among those who, under normal circumstances, he would have called enemies: Whites and people from other Indigenous ethnic groups, who taught him how to drink manioc beer. The first daughter of Paletó and To'o, Orowao Karaxu, born before contact, was still a girl when they arrived in Sagarana. She grew up there, became a young woman, and, her breasts having only recently developed, she married Orowao Kun, already separated from Xatoji and a widower of his second wife. Soon after, the couple returned to the Negro River.

Paletó lived in Sagarana for many years before returning to the Negro River. "I spent a long time there, my daughter, a long time!" Abrão, today fifty years old, was born in Sagarana, as well as our sister Main Tawi. Our three younger siblings—A'ain Tot, Davi, and Ja—were born later on the Negro River. While To'o breastfed Abrão, A'ain Kaxun, Paletó's brother, the one who shot an arrow into the arm of a White man in the episode of contact, became a widower. To'o adopted his daughter Niro, giving one breast to her and the other to Abrão. Later, their sister Wem Xu came from the Negro River to fetch the niece and take her with her, which caused To'o enormous pain. According to Paletó, she cried for days on end.

I met Niro on the Negro River, living with her father, her aunt Wem Xu, the latter's husband, and the children from the second marriage of A'ain Kaxun, who had also been widowed. She is a strong young woman with short hair and a fringe, Wari' style, and dimples that catch the eye when she laughs. Recently we experienced a tense and sad moment together. We went to visit her younger brother, Nelson, in the Guajará-Mirim prison, where he had been jailed for some months, unjustly accused of rape by the Christian father of a young Wari' woman from another village. All the family had moved to Guajará to be closer to Nelson, despite being too afraid to visit him in jail. My sisters had asked me not to say anything about Nelson to Paletó, who was spending a few days in the city at that moment. He was fragile and, my sisters said, would not be able to bear the news.

I arranged with my friend Gil, who occasionally went to the prison as part of the support work provided by the Catholic Church, for us to visit Nelson, and we passed by the family's house to invite them to go with us. The father and aunt continued to lack the courage to see the young man in that situation, but Niro wanted to go with us. We arrived there, were searched, and they ordered Nelson to be fetched. He arrived handcuffed, his head bowed, which provoked a fit of sobbing from Niro. Afterwards, they sat side by side and began to talk in a low voice, in the Wari' way. Some days later, after we visited the courts in search of documents with the help of a lawyer friend from the Public Prosecutor's Office, it became clear that the accusation did not stand up and that Nelson's rights had been violated. He was released shortly thereafter.

Hearing reports that Orowao Kun had struck his daughter Orowao Karaxu, Paletó returned for the first time to his native land, accompanied by his small son, Abrão, then called Wem Xain. Paletó hitched a ride as far as Guajará with a worker from Sagarana called Paulo. From there, he was taken to the Negro River on the boat of the Evangelical missionary Abílio, who lived there for many years. At that time, the Wari' were no longer living at Barracão Velho. The former SPI had been abolished in 1967 and replaced by Funai, which, in 1972, founded a new base, a little above the confluence of the Negro and the Pacaás Novos, where the Rio Negro-Ocaia Post is situated today. Paletó tells that, accustomed as he was to the large plantations of banana and manioc in Sagarana, on arriving he was astonished by the small size of the gardens there, even the maize crops, realizing that the Wari' on the Negro were unfamiliar with these cultigens.

On meeting him, Orowao Kun, his son-in-law, immediately announced that he was a believer in God, to which Paletó replied: "Why do you believe in God? You believe in nothing. If at least you could see God!" Royal, the missionary, went to see him, speaking their language fluently, calling him brother and referring to the boy Wem Xain, in Wari' style, as "our son." It was Royal who gave him the new name, the name of "our grandfather," Royal explained, the man who long ago believed in God. Paletó initially did not like it, but in the end Abrão (Abraham) kept his new name.

Having cleared up the issue with his son-in-law, and back once more in Sagarana, Paletó joined forces with those unhappy with the living conditions there and wished to move away to live somewhere distant from the mission base. The opportunity soon arrived: a large fire burned down the refectory, and some families took the chance to flee. Paletó, To'o, and their two children were among them. They went to settle far upriver, in a locality that for a long time was known as "Paletó's garden." More years passed there until he returned to the Negro River for good.

I discovered an interesting passage from the book of an anthropologist who lived in Sagarana between 1969 and 1970:

> The most powerful family head at Sagarana was Paletó. His position of influence was somewhat extraordinary, according to all my civilized and Indian informants. He was a man of middle-age, capable and diligent as a hunter and farmer. His knowledge of traditional mythology and ritual was unsurpassed, but it was primarily his reputation for supernatural power that accounted for his status. He drew a large number of younger men to his settlement and he initiated two or three *chicha* feasts held during my stay in the field. Members from his group all indicated that it was he who "ordered" the *chicha* to be made. . . . When he moved out of the mission settlement, his brother and family and four younger men and their families moved with him.*

Paletó clearly was long recognized among his people as a great man.

---

* Bernard von Graeve, *The Pacaa Nova: Clash of Cultures on the Brazilian Frontier* (Ontario: Broadview Press, 1989), 69.

19.
BECOMING A BELIEVER

WHEN WEM XU went to fetch her baby niece Niro in Sagarana, other people from the Negro River went with her
and told the Wari' there that they had become believers. They
said that God had created everything, and that he was watching
them. Paletó tells that the Wari' who had left the Negro River
at the start of their religious instruction, when they still did
not understand what the missionary Royal was talking about,
found the conversation of the visitors very strange.

He recalled that as evening approached, the Wari' visitors summoned the people from Sagarana: "Come all of
you, come hear the word of God." They continued: "Don't
smoke, don't screw other women, don't steal." Paletó angrily
retorted: "Why are you believers for no reason? Go to your
own homes, your wives are waiting there! Those claiming to
be believers must be there screwing your wives." They sang,
"Let's follow Jesus to heaven," and told the people from
there: "The priest who lives with you here believes in stone.
He sculpts the stone and says it is your God. True believers
don't believe in stone."

What finally led Paletó to declare himself a believer, he
said, was fear of the end of the world; more specifically, fear

of being abandoned by his countryfolk and kin, many of them believers since the end of the 1960s, and who would therefore go to heaven. What would happen to those who remained on earth, Royal said, according to Paletó, would be reminiscent of a horror film: "If you don't believe, you'll stay on earth and the jaguar will eat you. There will be all kinds of animal spirits. An enormous cricket will eat the Wari'. An enormous cricket sent from heaven. God will send it to eat all the nonbelievers." Paletó went fishing with Abrão, heard a thunderclap, and was frightened the world would end. "We were very scared," Paletó said. Rather than being enchanted with the idea of heaven—envisaged as a somewhat bland place where everyone is equal, no sex or festivals take place, and people drink water, eat bread, and spend the whole time writing—it was the fear of hell that drove the Wari' toward God. There they would burn forever, their skin full of sores, and feel an extreme thirst that could never be quenched.

On returning home after this fishing trip, Paletó told his wife To'o that he wanted to be a believer. At first she disliked the idea, but after a while decided to accompany her husband and both of them went to the pastor's house to announce their decision. On the day of the service, they made their announcement to everyone else, and some time later they were baptized, dipped in the water of the Negro River. According to Paletó, To'o's baptism did not go well; the fact that some time later she had sex with another man proved, as they had suspected, the immersion in water had been insufficient, since at the time they saw that the hair on top of her head remained dry.

Some years later, by now at the start of the 1980s, a short time before I met him, Paletó had become involved in war

club fights and, as they say, quit God. The same happened
with most of the Wari' in the first years of the same decade.
He went back to being a believer when he was older, in 2001:
"I returned to God. Today, I believe properly. I'm old. Old
people don't live long." "Be a believer so that your double
stays well. Your wife too, they said to me." According to
some people who also became believers again in 2001, this
reconversion happened when they watched the airliner attack
on the World Trade Center on the community television.
Based on the explanation of the event by the pastors, they
thought that a world war was about to break out, a sure sign
that the end of the world was approaching.

A moment of collective revivalism had occurred earlier,
but it did not involve Paletó and the inhabitants of the Negro
River. In 1994, a slight earthquake shook the Ribeirão Post
region and led its inhabitants, who were living in a "pagan
phase" like the other Wari', to reconvert immediately. When
I arrived in the region about six months after the quake, I
heard diverse accounts of it and of people's reactions. According to one woman living at the Lage Post, around an hour
by car from Ribeirão, the earth shook there too in the late
afternoon, and pans fell from the shelves. Frightened, some
people ran to the house of the missionary Teresa, who told
them about the end of the world and the return of Jesus. On
the Negro River, Paletó and my sister Orowao Karaxu offered
me another version rich in details: the people from Ribeirão
had become believers again because of the earthquake, when
a cloud parted and fire emerged, and then the water began to
well out of the ground (as in the Wari' flood myth). As the
water rose, they left their houses and shouted, asking Jesus
to wait for them to become believers.

When I arrived on the Negro River in January 2002, various people asked me for news about the world war and questioned me directly on whether the Taliban had reached Rio de Janeiro. There were no more missionaries living on the Negro River, and unaware that they had turned into Christians, I had no clear idea of what was happening. Nor was I conscious of the almost nightly evening services at the local church. At that time, the church was located in a stilt palm house with a thatch roof, some distance from the school where my children and I were staying. There, I was visited by Paletó almost every day, but at a certain time he would leave, with some evasive explanation or other, turning down my invitation to dine with us. This surprised me because he made the same decision even when I offered him his favorite meal: spaghetti bolognese. That was when I discovered he did not want me to know he was frequenting church, fearing my disapproval. Now aware of what was happening, I began to join these services and converse a lot with the Wari' about God, whom they called "the truly invisible one," about Jesus, His son, and about the Holy Ghost, God's "double."

By frequenting the church services, I made Paletó happy, concerned as he was with my salvation and going to heaven. This would save him, already himself in heaven, from having to refuse my requests for water in hell, which for them is also situated up in the sky, just beside heaven. Although I always explained that I was attending the church services out of curiosity about their life and not to become a believer myself, he would grin broadly when he saw me enter, displaying the pride Christian parents feel when their children resolve to "follow God." Consequently, Paletó's initial uneasiness about my opinion did not last long, and I have a photo of him beside me in which he is wearing a pink T-shirt with the following slogan emblazoned on the front: *Jesus nosso caminho*, Jesus our path. On his head, he wore the black-and-white-checked wool hat that my father in Rio had sent to him. His expression is serious, mine smiling, a pumpkin-colored shirt and a Peruvian wool bag crossed over my shoulder, in which I always carried my small notebook, pen, mosquito repellent, and a little flashlight.

In these services, conducted by the Wari' pastors entirely in their own language, they sang, and still sing, Christian hymns translated from English and Portuguese into Wari' by the missionaries and their Indigenous assistants, pray in admiration of the divine work of creation, ask God for protection, and study the Bible books already translated. These services are so long, especially on Sunday mornings, that some worshippers, especially older people, fall asleep and have to be woken up by the deacons, who wander around the church ensuring observance of good behavior. When André was small, I once asked Francisco, then eleven years old, to attend the service with me to help take care of his brother. Accustomed to having fun playing with the Wari' children, who would run about with their bows simulating wars with the enemies, in the case of André, or accepting the challenge to play chess, in the case of Francisco, the boys became very bored. Francisco eventually declared: "I'll do anything you ask me, but I won't come to church ever again." This did not prevent them him learning some Brazilian versions of Christian hymns with friends his age, especially one that tells repeatedly of a small sheep that has strayed from the flock, bleating "baa, baa."

Although completely opposed to the work of religious conversion, I was always respectful of the choice of the Wari'. This did not stop me, though, from explaining my reasons for not being a believer, even though this caused Paletó some consternation. Even so, however much I tried to explain myself, the fact that I frequented the church was a clear sign in the opposite direction: in his view, I was indeed becoming a believer, especially considering that actions are, for them, much more important than words. And in fact I was in the church.

But they knew I had other interests too. One time, by now in 2014, a very old man called Oro Iram was visiting the Negro River, staying in the house of his granddaughter, my friend Topa'. The pastor Awo Kamip, at the end of the service, told me to go and chat with this man since he had dreamed of animals in human form, a topic of interest to me. However much they had been catechized by fundamentalist

missionaries, who insist on a single worldview, the one expressed literally by the words of the Bible, the Wari' seem to be naturally molded to accept a multiplicity of views. They are radically nondogmatic.

Beto, my former husband, reminded me recently of an episode that occurred in Rio de Janeiro in 1993. He had taken Abrão and Paletó to Santos Dumont Airport to see the aircraft taking off and landing. Paletó first saw a small airplane and observed that it had flown only because it was small. He doubted that bigger ones could do the same. So they waited for a large airplane to take off and, responding to Beto's look of "see?", he said, "*That one* flew!", implying that he did not automatically assume such a capacity would be valid for any other airplane.

Some services include confessions in which the person goes to the front of the church and says simply: "I fell in with the Devil." In the past, Paletó told me, the confession, also made publicly, went into details about the sin. Since this very often involved adultery, it provoked innumerable fights. There are also the testimonies of the new believers, who stand in front of the church as a group and announce that they have decided to follow God. Those present then ask: "Truly?" If the positive response is sufficiently emphatic, they approach this group of people standing still in front of everyone and shake their hands, Brazilian style. Once a month the Holy Supper takes place, where people eat chunks of wheat bread made by women, which for the occasion they call *pamonha*, maize cake, and drink small cups of grape juice, brought from the city. Not everyone can eat and drink, only those who have confessed publicly, or privately to one of the pastors.

In 2005 I found out that Paletó had learned to "see the paper," as the Wari' describe learning to read. We were in his house, which at the time was at Linha 26, and Ja, my younger sister, told me the news. My curiosity was piqued, and I asked Paletó to read something to me of his own choice from one of the Christian "lesson books"—booklets produced by the missionaries with the help of Wari' translators. Paletó opened a page and began to read the text, running along the line with his fingers, just like the pastors in the church. I noted that there were differences in the words, but the content of what he said was the same as on the paper. I quickly understood that Paletó had memorized the text and, for him, and for his daughter Ja who had been to school and was literate, the difference between knowing what was written on the paper and actually reading what was written there had not the slightest importance. Paletó was "seeing the paper" and that was what mattered; knowing the exact words was not an issue for the Wari'. As he got older, Paletó said that he had been left unable to read as he could not see well because his eyes were tired, the same thing that happened to various other older people. To the Wari', reading was a capacity of the body, of the eyes, and not of the mind or the brain.

20.
ONE COACH STATION, TWO AIRPORTS, AND A TITANIUM LEG

FOR ME, the father-daughter relation between Paletó and myself was mainly constructed in our journeys together, especially on his trips to Rio de Janeiro in 1992, 2009, and 2012. The same applies to my sibling relation with Abrão, who accompanied our father on the three voyages he made to my house, as well as once coming alone, when he had a medical problem in 2008.

I have a precise memory of the scene of them arriving each time. The first was at the Rio coach station, accompanied by Evanir, a teacher from the Rio Negro-Ocaia Post who was traveling to visit her family in the South and was kind enough to accompany them as far as Rio. It was only a short time since I had seen them as I had been on the Negro River with Francisco a few months back. While waiting for them to arrive, I had spent the preceding days getting ready to welcome them, setting up what would be their *tapit*, or bed, on a sofa bed located on the veranda of my house in the neighborhood of Laranjeiras, next to a large glass window wall, which provided a view of the street below and the surrounding mountains. I soon discovered that what to me was a beautiful view was, to them, terrifying. I lived on the

fourth floor, and being so high up they were scared that the wind would smash my apartment block.

I made *chicha* with the maize I had bought at the market: I grated it, processed it with water in the blender, sweetened it, and left it ready to offer them as soon as they passed through the doorway, just as the Wari' do when welcoming kin at home. On that hot December day, I left for the bus station in the morning in my navy-blue Fiat Uno. Beto and Francisco, then two years old, stayed at home waiting. Later I wrote in my notebook:

> At 10am I went to pick them up at the bus station. Paletó standing still, next to Abrão and Evanir, at the front entrance, a colorful Bolivian bag slung over his shoulder. I spoke first with Evanir who was in front. When I went to speak with Paletó, he hugged me; afterwards, he pointed to his son, as though reminding me not to forget to hug him too. Everyone in the Fiat, we head to my home. I point out the apartment buildings and tell Paletó that the Whites live on top of each other, right to the top. He replies saying that they are probably descendants of the OroTaoPa, a mythic people.

The second time, in August 2009, they arrived at Galeão (now Tom Jobim) Airport, and Paletó used a hospital mask, which I had asked people in Porto Velho to give him and Abrão, since we were in the middle of a swine flu epidemic, and I was worried about contamination on the airplane. He took off the mask to speak to me and laughed at my worry. It was the first time Paletó had flown, although he had entered a parked airplane on his first trip to Rio. I was curious to know what he had thought, whether he had felt afraid. He just said that he could make a home for himself inside the airplane, the same observation he had made on entering the Sugarloaf Mountain cable car, and a subway car seventeen years earlier.

The third time, in December 2012, it had been three years since I had seen him. Over those years, I had tried several times to get them come to visit me. Once I had even bought them plane tickets, but for various reasons they had resisted the visit. On this third visit, they arrived at Santos Dumont Airport. Concerned when they failed to emerge from the baggage reclamation area, I begged the guard to let me look inside. On seeing Paletó, I was startled by the amount he had aged. His hand trembled, and he was thinner and bent over. At that moment, I thought about the huge responsibility I had assumed in asking him to travel so far. But I soon relaxed as Paletó started joking about everything he saw, was incredibly good humored, and walked well, albeit slowly. In the end, his stay in Rio was like a spa break for him: he ate heartily, became fatter, slept well, and was examined by a doctor, who medicated him for Parkinson's. After that I sought to ensure that Paletó always received the drugs in the village, sent by the FUNASA (National Health Foundation) pharmacy.

There was also the one time that Abrão came alone, in 2008. I had visited the Negro River in January that year and, on arrival, I encountered Abrão on crutches, with no movement in one of his legs. On seeing me, he began to cry, and told me about the boat accident in which a motor injured his leg. I saw little of him that month since I had dedicated the trip to making expeditions to traditional Wari' villages and spent most of my time traveling. On the day of my departure, at the beginning of February, when I went to his house to say goodbye, Abrão broke his silence and was startlingly direct compared to the roundabout way in which the Wari' invariably ask for something: "Either you take me with you or I shall die here!" We traveled together to Guajará-Mirim, from there to Porto Velho and then to Rio de Janeiro, where we began a pilgrimage through hospitals to find some kind of surgical treatment. It was not a sightseeing trip like the others, since Abrão, finding it exceedingly difficult to move about, was deeply sad throughout. Sometimes I had to leave him at home, and I would return to find him sitting in silence in my living room, the television switched off. After a month, we finally found a solution. By chance I had mentioned Abrão's condition to a university colleague who had a medical student from a specialized orthopedic hospital. Luckily for us, the student conducted mobile orthopedic surgeries, including to the city of Porto Velho. Abrão's surgery was scheduled for August the same year, a titanium prosthesis was placed in his thigh, and he now walks normally. The only nuisance is when he passes metal detectors: on his return to Rio with Paletó the following year, I was almost expelled from Santos Dumont Airport when I tried to enter the embarkation area to explain why Abrão set off the alarm as he passed through the detector.

21.
WHERE THE WATER MEETS THE CLOUDS AND THE FISH-MEN

MY MEMORIES of December 1992 include Francisco, very small, dancing to the sound of the little harmonica that Paletó played for him, the Laranjeiras home with its beautiful view, and the end-of-year heat in Rio—not, though, anything like the heat of the present. Over their bed, next to the window, on a kind of closed veranda that was a continuation of the living room, a ceiling fan spun.

Before this, Paletó and Abrão had never traveled beyond the small city of Guajará-Mirim, where there were no apartment blocks, elevators, or tunnels. None of these strange things seemed to surprise Paletó, however, and he immediately related them to mythic times and figures. Looking up at the lofty buildings, Paletó concluded: "The Brazil nut tree isn't tall!" Seeing a bulldozer in action, without catching sight of the driver, he remarked that the Whites had been wise not to laugh at objects that move on their own, since when the Wari' did so, they stopped moving, and today all the work has to be done by people themselves. I explained to him that there was a driver inside, but he did not appear to have found the information relevant. On the 2012 trip, from inside the car, he saw the automatic garage door of my building open, and not having spotted the remote control in my hand, he asked me whether the door had a "heart." In other words, thought, consciousness.

He was similarly nonchalant when I took them to the Rio-Sul shopping mall one day after their arrival. I imagined they would be impressed by the imposing structure, the many floors, the lighting, and also perhaps feel uncomfortable in the midst of it all. But instead they were intent on seeing everything and intrigued that there were other levels above and below us. When we glimpsed the second floor from the third, Paletó cautiously approached the balcony. Presuming that he would find the sight very odd, I remarked, "The Whites are crazy." He quickly responded, "It's good! The Whites know a lot."

In the recorded account that he made of this trip at my request, while still in Rio, addressed sometimes to me, sometimes to his kin back home (who would later hear the cassette tape), his memories were different from my own in

an interesting way. I thought about the episodes as sequential events, whereas Paletó recounted them focusing on the people present in each of the scenes, and on the food. In all the narrated scenes, he first had to specify the people present. He would ask Abrão: "Had Evanir already left? Was Francisco there too?"

His narrative begins with the three-day bus journey from Guajará-Mirim to Porto Velho, and Porto Velho to Rio, changing buses in Goiânia (the first bus continued on to São Luiz, the land of Josélio, a Funai employee, Paletó noted) with various stops on the way:

> We had breakfast. Midday, we passed by a cemetery, we got out, we bathed, we drank coffee and ate bread. I didn't think anymore [yearning for home], my thought disappeared; I just sat there. I saw all the towns. We got out again. We climbed back on again. Night fell and then the day dawned for us. We saw all the big plantations of the Whites, maize, beans, pineapple, rice. We don't know how to plant [he concluded]. The Whites make big plantations. Where does it end [the plantation], where does it end, where does it end? Very far. You will all say: "What you say isn't true!" But the end was very away, so far that we forgot people [the Wari']. We went and went, night came, and we slept. We arrived in a small town and got out, we drank coffee, we ate bread.

As well as the big plantations, what also impressed Paletó were the long deserted stretches, treeless and without houses or people. And he had a sense of distance previously unknown to him:

Road, road, without any city, without Whites. Very far. Very far. I spoke aimlessly here. We thought aimlessly. Wari' from Tanajura live there, Wari' of the Mamoré [River] live there, our heart said. When we really travel far, we no longer know where we are traveling. We [the Wari' as a whole] don't know what far means.

Paletó then spoke of the arrival in Rio:

Morning, no sun yet, we saw the outskirts of Rio. We thought that Evanir would leave us on the road and continue on her way. We then entered amid the many houses of the Whites. We entered further and further. We arrived and got out. We went up on the strange ground that unrolled [an escalator] and I was afraid of my foot entering there. Evanir held on to me; I was unable to stand still properly. Evanir said: "She will arrive, she likes you [both] a lot." And I said: "Where is she coming from?" It was like you were [animal] game, with me asking: "Where is she coming from? Where is she? Where is she?" I searched among the crowd of Whites. I searched. And then I saw her: she looked like Wari'. You arrived. "We're going to enter the hole [tunnel], father," she told me. It seemed like I was going to die [in the tunnel]. My body went cold. I was unable to breathe: "I'm going to die, I'm going to die!" I don't know who the person is who digs these holes.

After we parked in my apartment block garage, another hole, we entered the elevator, which Paletó thought was a small room and was startled when it began to rise, and further unnerved by the shudder as it arrived: "It seemed like it had broken, split, it seemed like it would plummet." But the next day, he already liked the elevator a lot and always went up on it, even though Abrão, fearful, sometimes preferred the stairs. The astonishments were many on this first day. When I showed him the bathroom, Paletó looked to the sides and above, and asked me where the leaves were. I showed him the roll of toilet paper and convinced him to treat it like leaves.

I went to the kitchen and poured the *chicha* into two cups, which I then proudly served, saying the right words for the occasion: "Here is your *chicha*, my father!" The two of them drank it straight down, the Wari' way. I was surprised that this moment of the *chicha*, which, I imagined, would catch their attention or make them laugh, was absent from the narratives. He did not even remember the *chicha* that I made, perhaps precisely because it seemed so commonplace, too everyday to merit being mentioned to others.

On the same day, I took them to the beach so that they could see the ocean for the first time. On the sand, they stood looking at the sea in wonder. Paletó tasted the water to see if it was salty (*wita*, which is the same word for sweet). He also tasted the wet sand and then the dry sand. He put a little in his mouth and spat it out. He was surprised by the taste. He did not want to go in the water, arguing that he was not hot. Abrão entered and swam easily, diving in the waves. Paletó observed: "That damned boy has no fear of the water." Evanir told me afterward that Abrão told her he was the first Wari' to enter the sea. At night, speaking on the telephone with Orowao Kun, Paletó's son-in-law, and João, a young Wari' man, who were at the Casa do Índio (Indian Infirmary) in Guajará, Abrão said that what I told them was true, the water really is salty and one cannot see where it ends.

Paletó's narrative of this moment has a special flavor:

> Soon we went out again. We're going to see the sand! Abrão soon went into the water. It's very wild water. The Mamoré [River] is very small. People think they're going to sink. Ha! [mocking those afraid of sailing on the Mamoré] It's a stream. There it's a big water. It seems like the water merges with the clouds, you can't see where it flows out, you can't see the end. We were embarrassed by the women with no clothes. You could see their [pubic] hair. The clothing entered their ass. They felt no shame. They only covered their breasts. You could see the edges of their vagina.

The absence of clothes of the women on the beach drew Paletó's attention every time he was in Rio. That was unusual, since Wari' men and women had, until the recent past, no problems with nudity when among themselves, although they always sought to shield their nudity from the gaze of Whites, including my own. Paletó explained: "If I had already seen the vagina of a [White] woman!"

We went many other times to the beach, and I recall one day we saw a vendor using a headband with a fake knife sticking out from the middle of his forehead. Paletó was stunned that the man could still manage to walk, speak, and laugh, and we had to buy one of these headbands for him. Another day, later in the afternoon, I left him and Abrão on the beach, already quite empty, for half an hour while I went to the bank. When I came back, they were nowhere. I became desperate, asking everyone around whether they had seen two "Indians." Some said yes, others no, but there was no sign of them. Some time later they reappeared, smiling, precisely at the spot where I had left them, saying that they had gone for a short walk.

It was on discovering the beach that Paletó finally understood why we were White: the sea had eaten our skin. I then reminded him of the Black people we had also seen there: "I don't know!" he replied, without, however, thinking that this rendered his association invalid. He would probably find an additional explanation for Black skin.

The Wari' sense of direction always surprised me, even more so in the city, where I presumed that they would become disoriented. As soon as we arrived in my home, they went to the window and examined the landscape at length,

marking high points as a reference. One day, calling to speak to Abrão at home, I discovered that he had gone out alone to walk, returning tranquilly some hours later. In the busy streets, however, they remained glued to me, walking right behind in single file, as though on a forest track, even when I insisted on us walking side by side. I imagined that the packed streets bothered them, and one afternoon, walking down Nossa Senhora de Copacabana Avenue, I decided to take a detour through some less busy side streets, certain that it would be a relief for them. A few minutes later, Paletó asked me why we did not go back to where there were so many Whites that the smell of people so closely packed, rubbing against him, stuck to his skin:

> They're like the *koka* fish that bump against our legs when we go weir fishing [where the fish are corralled into a stretch of river emptied of water by a dam]. There are too many to catch. Peccaries are numerous, but Whites are far more.

I had many similar surprises. In the middle of their stay, friends loaned us a house in a mountainous area on the way to Friburgo in a place called Sibéria, surrounded by forests, with no electricity or running water. Beto, Francisco, Abrão, Paletó, and I went. Our intention was to spend at least three days there, returning to Rio on Monday evening, allowing them a break from the city and its noise and light. A kind of return to forest. We came back early, on Sunday, when we realized how much they suffered from the cold and missed the city. As soon as we had arrived there, Paletó asked me: "Where's the crowd, the cars?"

He described the voyage in his recorded narrative:

We went very far. We crossed a bridge over very large water. We climbed up. They were many Whites, many Whites, until there were no more Whites, only path. We drove up, the path was bad, the rock very steep. The car drove aimlessly. Aparecida and I and the boy Francisco rode. Beto and Abrão walked. We reached a small stream and the car was unable to pass. A man felt sorry for us and helped, we pushed. We continued climbing. We arrived. Beto and Abrão arrived. Then the real cold arrived. We felt very cold. "Let's take a bath!" It was impossible to take a bath. Very cold [the water]. You too would not bathe with this cold water from this other land. "Let's make a fire [in the wood stove]!" They gave us blankets. The next day: "Let's cut firewood to roast the fish." I took the Whites' axe, cut the wood, but I cut my leg. I struck myself! My head hurt. "I'm very cold!" I said. "We won't wait until Monday, let's go!" Beto said. "If you didn't feel so cold!" On the way back, we stopped at a trout farm. We went to see the fish. We wanted to see the fish that the Whites breed. They weren't few in number. A lot of fish. There's an image [photo] of there. Many places with fish, small and large. There were some small ones, like leporinus. The fish bred by the Whites were like chickens. We took photos. We gathered a fish with a strange gathering thing [a dip net]. We saw a strange jaguar [a Siamese cat] which looked like a capuchin monkey.

In the end: "We climbed the rock, we came down [the mountains, along the road] and then there was sunshine. Our heart was cheered. Really bad, that forest there."

While they liked the city and the large number of people who lived there, they never ceased to be surprised by this, and Paletó very often asked me why I did not greet the people who passed me on the street. He was astonished when I said that I did not know these people. "How can you not?" he asked. "How can you live in the same place without knowing each other?" Some years later, on recollecting this, he concluded: "We are kin to each other. We're not like you who are kin only to your younger brother, Dudu, your father, your mother. You like each other for no good reason. Why don't you make yourselves kin too?" To his people back home, he said: "Here there are so many people that we are no longer Wari'. We are like Whites. We become lost [among the multitude]. The Whites look at us, look at our Aparecida. She is not ashamed to speak in Wari'. They look at my [perforated] ear and recognize that I am Wari'." At other moments, he was careful to classify all the Whites of the city as Wari', recognizing their humanity, and not as *wijam*, enemies, as he always had done. It was also a way of feeling safe in a strange environment. One day, still in Rio, he remarked: "The Wari' used to say they would kill the Whites, but they have no idea just how many Whites there are. If they killed them, the Whites would kill them all."

He constantly thought of new reasons why there were so many Whites, until one day, as we were strolling in Paineiras, in the Tijuca Forest, he saw many people running, lots of them women accompanied by their dogs. "Finally I understand," he said to me ironically, "you have sex with these animals and that's why you reproduce so quickly; you screw the dogs, sucking their genital organs, penis and vagina, and then you have dog children." On another occasion, he saw an elderly man carrying a cat and said: "They screw cats. That's why there are so many Whites. They are jaguar children." "That's why they fly," he said about Whites, referring to the men who bungee-jumped from great heights, as he had seen on television. Joking, he speculated about everything that made a big impact on him.

I note that, back in 1993, when he narrated the voyage to his kin, Paletó referred to me as Aparecida, or "our Aparecida," and not as daughter, or our daughter, in Wari' style, as he came to call me over the rest of his life. In the final years, he rarely pronounced my name, always calling me "daughter," or, when he was in the company of his other children, calling us all "children": "Come here now and help me, children!" It really does seem that our kinship was constructed slowly by living together, sharing memories, and, above all, food. "We ate loads, loads," Paletó said to those who would hear the cassette-tape when back in the village.

I imagine what it must have been like for them to see this abundance of food that was repeated day after day. In the village, food might be plentiful for a day or two, but then scarcer, since there was no way at that time to prevent food from going bad; thus, people ate as much as they could of what there was at the moment, as though to produce a reserve in anticipation of the days of shortage. In Rio, we went out to the supermarket together and bought beef and chickens, saying among ourselves that we had gone hunting. Everything we put on the table was finished then and there, which left me happy to have provided them with food they liked.

Only later, when accompanying them to a friend's birthday party, did I realize that there was more at work in this "licking the plate" than hunger or an atavistic response to food insecurity. It was a chic party in a big apartment in Ipanema, and I had bought new clothes for Paletó and Abrão, who dressed in trousers, shirts, and shoes. At their request, they also used perfume. They were the hit of the party, with people asking them the most bizarre things about the life of "Indians." My friend with the birthday kindly offered Paletó a glass of Coca-Cola, which he downed at once. My friend smiled, happy that he was pleasing him, and went immediately to fetch another glass, which again was drunk immediately. After a third glass, Paletó began to burp and I perceived that he would vomit if he continued drinking. I asked him if he wanted to stop, and he asked me back: "Can I?" I then understood that Paletó was drinking Coca-Cola like *chicha* in a Wari' festival, offered by the hosts to guests in large gourds, and necessarily drunk straight down. To be able to drink the many gourds, the guest must vomit now and then, and this is what Paletó was getting ready to do, out of respect for good party manners and a good relationship with his host. What is offered cannot be refused.

Partly because of these persistent misunderstandings, partly, I hope, out of pleasure, Paletó and Abrão fattened so much in these two months spent in Rio that I had to buy new clothes for them since those we bought initially for the visit no longer fit. However, when, during the first few days, Evanir remarked that they would get fat, Paletó immediately replied: "I'll fatten up when I return to the Negro River," clearly signaling who his true kin were. Following the other trips, though, he began to recognize in front of his Wari' kin that he ate a lot at my house and became fat. Jokingly, he threatened them, saying that if they did not treat him well there, he would come back to live with me and die in Rio, so that only two of his grandchildren would weep for him: Francisco and André.

22.

THE ANIMALS WHO ARE PEOPLE, THE BIG ROCK, AND THE BONES OF THE DEAD

I N THE NARRATIVE of his 1992–93 visit, Paletó recalled the day we went to the zoo:

The day arrived for us. We're going to see things! We entered another hole, very large [the Rebouças Tunnel]. I've no idea who digs these holes. A large hole. We emerged. We went to the animals. Beto paid [for the entry tickets]. We saw jaguars, bears, camels [Abrão, by his side, helped him remember the names of the animals], strange animals, a strange jaguar [tiger], a strange spider monkey [chimpanzee]. It looked like Wari', a real person, it ate sitting down. That strange animal that goes up and up, a giraffe. A tall, tall animal, you can't reach its head. It ate food there high above. A strange bird [rhea]. Big, very big. Taller than Wari'. It's hairless. It only has a little [hair], none on its belly. A really large bird. There were animals we recognized and others we didn't. We saw the true deer, our deer. Agouti, our agouti. Spider monkey, but it wasn't the same as ours. We went to see the strange animals, a house of bats.

I remember this visit clearly. Francisco was very small, and now and then he would tire and have to be carried in a backpack-like infant carrier, made of turquoise blue canvas, which we had taken for this purpose. He was just as fascinated by the zoo, but it was not his first time there. Back then, in 1992, the Wari' had no television or any access to photos or images of animals from other regions, save for some schoolbooks that showed bears and tigers to illustrate letters of the alphabet. They were astonished not only by the strangeness of the animals but also by the existence of a park with animals displayed in cages. Paletó was puzzled by the fact that we kept animals there for no reason, given that I had explained to him they would not be eaten. "So why catch them?" He asked me whether the hippopotamus was a tapir, calling it "water spirit," and, like Abrão, was amazed to see it defecate and rub its dirty rear against the wall. Abrão, Paletó told me, was afraid of seeing this scene again in his sleep.

What particularly struck me was the reaction of the Wari' to a couple of chimpanzees. They had never seen great apes before and the couple behaved in a very human way, the female picking nits off her husband, who from time to time would leave, fetch some straw, and place it on the covered part of the cage, making what seemed to be the couple's bed. Paletó asked me: "Are they people [*wari'*]? Do they speak?" In his various other narratives about this trip, he always emphasized the encounter with animals who were people, who picked nits, who made beds. Although they knew that many animals were in fact people, since the shamans always spoke about this and Paletó himself once had a jaguar mother-in-law, they had never seen them act like people in their animal form, as we had seen there at the zoo. This was the unusual aspect of the event, not any apparent sudden recognition of the tenuous boundaries between humanity and animality, which his remarks might seem to have emphasized. Paletó concluded this section of the narrative with an important observation: "We came back, and the food was ready. We ate. We ate a lot. We ate a lot of chicken. We didn't go hungry at all."

Paletó recalls that Evanir then left, as well as Gabriel, Beto's thirteen-year-old son, who had been spending a few days with us. On that day, he recounts, "We went swimming with Gabriel, his other son with another woman. He's grown up. I have a photo of him with his father."

The next day, another trip: "We didn't sit down [we didn't stay still]!" Paletó said.

> We're going to see the strange house on high! We arrived, we paid. We entered a little house that swung about a lot, swaying backwards and forwards. It seemed it would split in two. Aparecida held me by the arm. They weren't scared that it would split. We arrived on top. We saw cars below, very small, they looked like turtles to me. The people looked like small children. Now we're going really high! There was another vine that led there. We went up. High, truly high.

We were on Sugarloaf Mountain, via its famous cable car. Paletó says that this was the moment his fear dissipated and he began to breathe well in the city.

The trip to Corcovado (and the Christ the Redeemer statue) was much less exciting, since back then one could drive by car all the way to the top: "Let's go for a trip! Let's go

where God stays! There's a photo. We climbed really high. We
entered the clouds. It was as though it was small, I thought
unknowingly. It was very high." The last time we went there,
in 2012, accompanied by André, in a bad mood about being
roped into this tourist outing, they took away a mug with a
photo of them both as a souvenir. This time the image was not
kept by the Whites, as had happened with the plate on which
the vendor, on top of Sugarloaf, without their permission had
printed their photo to persuade them to buy it.

Some days later, I took them to see the National Museum, where I used to work and where I was then a doctoral
student in social anthropology. Two things impressed them:
the mummy and the human bones kept in wooden drawers
in the entrance lobby to some of the academic offices (they
were next to my office).

We're going to see the bones of the dead! We saw where
the skulls of the dead were. Many heads of dead people.
I was startled, I wanted to cry. If there was someone to
take the heads of these dead people! We saw a very ancient corpse, covered in paper [the mummy]. They rolled
him up and laid him out. It was the true body, not the
double. A true person. Bald, with the scalp from his head
torn. It wasn't the head of a monkey, but a Wari' head.
The feet were there, the scalp. Why don't you feel pity?
It's there that this one [referring to me] writes.

As we left, he said that the money I gave to the (informal)
parking attendant was to pay for the attendant's head, which
afterwards would be kept in the museum's drawers.

23.
THE SLIPPERY PEOPLE AND
THE BIG TELEVISION

PALETÓ'S NARRATIVE runs parallel to the jottings in my notebook. We went to a symphony concert in the Cecília Meireles Hall and Paletó was fascinated by the conductor, whom he called the chief. He kept saying that the conductor was the one who knew everything. When we came out, we saw there had been a rainstorm and the streets were full of water. We had to walk along the walls of the buildings, grabbing hold of the railings, while we looked down at the filth swilling around in the water below. As Paletó put it succinctly: "From the hole, we didn't hear the rain; the water rose and rose. There was shit floating in it. She said she was going to vomit. We yelled because of the rotten shit in the water."

From a visit to the Maracanã Stadium, where we saw the place from which emerged the "image of the voice [of the announcer]" on the radio, we headed to the nearby Maracanãzinho arena to see a skating show called *Holiday on Ice.*

"Let's go to the little Maracanã," Aparecida said. Beto stayed behind. We paid and sat down. Sit down here. They slid around. I don't know. How do they not die? How do they live? They have strange shoes. They run.

There were people inside an old trunk covered with leaves. And then came the really bizarre man. He raised the woman's foot. They spun around together. They ran together. Part of the body of one of them slipped inside the body of the other. We liked seeing the Whites being strange.

At Tivoli Park, an amusement park located by the lake: "Let's go out, let's see the train!" Paletó was impressed by the roller coaster, which he saw from outside, since only Abrão felt brave enough to enter:

It goes up and when it is at the top, the head faces down, and it descends. How do the people not die? If you, old show-offs [addressing his countryfolk], went up there, you would die. I don't show off for nothing, and that's why I didn't die. I saw our son with his head upside-down. Abrão cried. Francisco played on the little carousel. We entered the strange airplane, which went round and round. My eyes became dizzy. The dizziness got me! Beto said: "Let's go on the slide." "Okay," I said. Toboggan. We waited for those going up. We went up and we arrived at the top. There were many irons [toboggans] that came down. It's very slippery. It was very high. The ground was there below. Beto said: "Hold tight!" But he soon slid. I tried to hold on, but I slid too.

There was also their first time at the movies. Beto took Paletó and Abrão, along with his son Gabriel, to see a Western. Paletó was impressed that inside the movie theater it was completely night and yet afterwards, outside, it was day. "It was very dark, which is why we thought we would die. The doubles [images] of the Whites appeared, the double of the wind. Which is why we thought we would die." When they arrived back home, Paletó said he was feeling very cold. I discovered that the film was set in a cold and very windy place, and that Paletó said, in the middle of the film, that he felt very cold. As soon as he arrived, he lay down, rolled himself up in a blanket, and only broke his silence to tell me that when Francisco grew up, I should not let him join the army, so that he would not be killed (probably referring to the killings he saw in the Western).

The Wari' relation with television is interesting, since the idea of fiction with images was completely strange to them. At the moment when images, bodies, are seen, for them the event is really happening. When, at the end of the 1990s, they installed a television in a communal house at the Rio Negro-Ocaia Post, I accompanied the Wari' in their discoveries and questions. I remember that in January 2002 there was a soap opera called *O Clone* (The Clone), whose lead character was named Jade. Very often they asked me if I knew her (not the actress, but the character) and whether I had met her in Rio. I tried to explain to them numerous times that these people studied their lines on paper, and repeated them in front of a camera. But they did not seem to understand. One day, watching the soap opera with them, I saw the perfect opportunity to explain it. A pregnant woman, who in the episode the day before had a small belly, appeared that night with a huge one. So I said to them: "Look at that! How could a belly grow like that from one day to the next if it was true?" Immediately a woman replied: "Do you think we don't know that you Whites have medicines for everything?

Without doubt you also have a medicine to make the belly grow quickly." At home, watching television, I laughed at Paletó's very pertinent but unusual observations. Paletó remarked that he did not like seeing the Japanese animation with lots of fighting because he felt sorry for their doubles (who fought so much). Afterwards he asked me: "Don't they stop to eat?" Another day, after watching a morning program with Francisco, he commented that he did not like Xuxa, a famous TV show presenter, because she always spoke in a strange way, out of the side of her mouth. He found it very strange that she treated a piece of rubber (the plastic dolls she advertised in the shows) like real children.

Twenty years later, in December 2012, André took them to the cinema to see *Life of Pi*. Although they were already used to television by then, present in many houses on the

Negro River, a 3D film was something completely new. André told me that Paletó removed his glasses several times, startled, and that when the tiger jumped on Pi, he ducked and used the seatback in front of him as a shield.

On the last trip here, they asked me to take them to tour the Globo TV studios. Not knowing anyone who worked there, I remembered a colleague from my doctoral course who was a scriptwriter for one of the broadcaster's programs. He kindly put me in touch with the program team, who not only invited us to visit them but also sent a car to fetch us. On arrival, there was a dressing room with the sign "anthropologist and Indians," comfortably arranged with a sofa, water, and coffee, and a valet who asked us whether we wanted

Paletó reenacting funerary cannibalism with a doll,
in Beto's house, Itacoatiara, 2009

our clothes ironed. Paletó was wearing a black linen jacket belonging to Francisco. We went to have lunch in a canteen full of actors and, sitting next to Paletó, several times I had to contain my laughter at his comments. As they served us passion fruit mousse, Paletó told me, in Wari', that it looked like cum, at the same time as people next to us asked me whether he was enjoying it. We were taken in an electric cart to the soap opera sets, and the three of us were astounded by the quality of the fake objects: breads, cakes, even horse shit, from a period soap opera, which, they told us, was made from tea leaves. We saw a scene being filmed and headed to a live set with lots of music and scantily clad dancers. The chilly air conditioning did not allow us to stay long, though, as Paletó began to feel cold. The driver was waiting for us at the door.

24.
MAKING KIN

THE FIRST PERSON from my Rio family whom Paletó met was my maternal grandfather, Manoel. Ninety years old, his lungs failing, he was lying in his home in Santa Clara Street, in Copacabana, in a hospital bed with plastic oxygen tubes in his nose. However, he maintained his perennial good humor and wanted to meet the Wari' and talk with them. We sat, Paletó, Abrão, and I, in chairs by the side of his bed, which was raised so that he could sit. Grandad, as Paletó called him, told them about his childhood in the interior of Maranhão state, about his father's manioc plantation, which had to be watched to guard against marauding peccaries, and about his six or seven siblings fighting over the guava sweet made by their mother. Paletó loved the conversation, which I translated for him. Then, without hesitation, he asked whether my grandfather dreamed of my grandmother, who had died two years previously. When he shook his head, Paletó said to him: "So you're not going to die now!" My grandfather seemed to like the prediction and I explained to him that, for the Wari', deceased near kin tend to come in dreams to call on the sick person to join them.

Some days later we were invited to lunch at my parents' house. They liked the big living room, which Paletó praised: "It's long, it really looks like earth." He soon noted that I was the tallest of the family, and observed that Wari' women who lose their virginity later grow more; those who are "pierced for nothing" do not grow much. He was impressed by the fact that my mother cooked fish in a clay pot (a moqueca stew) and said to Beto: "I thought your mother-in-law wasn't Wari'." The very hot food made us sweat and Paletó remarked that we were like warriors. I assumed the comparison related to our use of forks, in that we ate with the same delicacy as warriors in seclusion, who use chopsticks to avoid dirtying their hands. "No," he told me, "it's not because of that. It's because the warriors drink hot *chicha* to sweat." He ate a lot and, to my parents' surprise, then left the table and lay down on the living room floor to rest.

My father Hélio later gave Paletó a shiny black baseball cap, which he immediately put on and thanked him, calling him older brother. Unbelievably, the cap was stolen that same day. He recounts the story in a recording:

> Her father gave me a hat that an American had given him. We ate. Let's go out! If only I had left my hat. I wore it and it disappeared rapidly. We went with Beto. I walked slightly apart from Beto and Abrão, and a man went by on a bicycle, hit my head and took the cap. Beto shouted: "They took his hat! Where did he go?" "He went that way!" I still dislike that White man. I wanted to kill him.

The hat was gone, but the relation between the two brothers—my two fathers—had already been made. Some weeks later, at the Christmas party at my parents' house, we sang Wari' *tamara* songs that we had rehearsed for the occasion at Paletó's insistence. Lacking the traditional drum of a ceramic base covered in rubber, which sets the rhythm to the music during festivals, we used a plastic ice cream container and a wooden spoon. Paletó then called his older brother to dance in line, as the Wari' do, and insisted that he play the drum. I shall never forget the image of the two dancing side by side, as well as many other images, from other visits, in which my fathers, unable to communicate verbally, embraced and sat next to each other.

My mother and Paletó had a special affection for each other, and I have a beautiful photo of the two with their heads touching, eyes closed and smiling. A memory of another Christmas, many years later, the same one when, moved by the tender scene, I photographed André with his head lying on Paletó's shoulder and one of his arms wrapped around his waist. In the photo both are smiling with their eyes closed. They are wearing identical checked shorts, which they had received as a present. That day, Paletó's hair was jet black since we had spent the previous afternoon dying it in my bathroom, at his request, with the toner he saw me using on my own hair. Sitting on the bidet, with Abrão and me standing next to him, he exclaimed that now he would appear young and attract looks from the young women. From the same period, I have a film in which Francisco, by now a young man, is lying in a hammock with Paletó, each with their head to one side, and each playing his flute, in a duet.

It was during the first Christmas, in 1992, that Paletó met my younger brother, Dudu, Mônica, his wife, and Luiz, their one-year-old son. That New Year, Dudu and Mônica rented an apartment in a hotel that faced the sea, in Copacabana, and invited us to celebrate together. We went down to the beach to see the fireworks, which at that time were set off directly from the sand, as well as the religious offerings and rituals. Men in drag drew the attention of Paletó, who went straight over to touch their breasts, to see whether they were real. Abrão argued with him, telling him to stop, saying that if he tried to touch the men he would end up in a fight. He recounts:

> The special day arrived, Christmas, on which we danced. Let's see the fire [fireworks]! We ate with your brother. We saw [on the beach] the small canoe [an offering pushed out to sea]. The believers arrived playing music, the countryfolk of Abílio [a missionary]. They sang. Those who believed, those who didn't believe, all stood around. They gave out paper, they gave some to me. Beto told us: "These are believers." Our brother Abílio lied when he said that the believers don't dance. Abílio didn't want us to dance. It went yellow, it went red, they were like arrows [the fireworks]. Pow!!! I liked them. I can't even tell you how many Whites there are! "We're going to see the shamans, the strange old woman," they told us. We made our way through lots of people. We held onto each other. We didn't see those who cured the Wari'. We only saw our grandmother, who imitated a turkey [he imitates her, referring to an older possessed woman in an Afro ritual]. The woman who smoked! I grabbed her by the arm. She looked at me strangely. Abrão said to me: "Don't hold the Whites because they

get angry." The light spun around. The woman who ate tobacco spun around and around, trembled, as though she was very cold.

Paletó found it natural that there existed shamans here too, with the difference that the animals that accompanied them, into which their doubles transformed, were different animals, such as the turkey, from the doubles of the Wari'. One day, when I took them with me to my yoga class, Paletó observed that the most flexible students probably had no bones. When I told him that Orlando, my teacher, who also taught a technique called bio-gymnastics, with animal movements, knew how to crawl, Paletó observed: "He's probably a shaman." Even I was considered a shaman when one day, on the Negro River, I offered to perform shiatsu on a man who had hurt himself in the forest. I had done a course and thought I could help. I just had not expected an enormous crowd of people to gather around me, which left me almost unable to continue. Fortunately, it seemed to work, and the man felt some relief. But they would not let me leave there before explaining what animal I accompanied. I did not know, and they were left to speculate whether I was a chicken or a cow.

Many other encounters happened between my sets of kin with their very different life histories, and I was always astonished how these people who did not speak a common language could communicate with such affection. I suspect that my family from Rio is as good at making kin as the Wari'. Dudu, Mônica, and their boys, years later, hosted Paletó and Abrão in Brasilia, and took them out to see the sights, including "Lula's house," the presidential residence. As well as my family, they met my friends here, in unusual encounters, in which they asked those who also worked with Indigenous peoples to speak words in the language and sing. They laughed a lot as they listened, and Paletó always talked about my luck in working with them, people who knew the right names for things, who called the moon moon, and the sun sun.

On one of his nights in Rio, Paletó dreamed that he was clearing undergrowth for a large airstrip at the Rio Negro-Ocaia Post. In the middle of analysis, I had a pseudo-Freudian moment and wrote in my field diary: "I think that he feels that he's opening up communication with the outside world, with the Whites." In a way, I was right—we were moving closer to each other, joining our villages and our lives.

Saying farewell to me at the coach station, at the end of his first trip, Paletó hugged me and said, referring to Francisco, who was two years old: "Don't waste our boy. Don't let him climb trees. Careful with the cars, so he can grow up."

25.
THE FAREWELL

Let's go father, let's go father!
Let's go father, let's go father!
My daughter said to me.
We went up high, really high.

— Song composed by Paletó about our visit to Sugarloaf Mountain,
Rio de Janeiro, December 13, 2012

A T THE START of December 2015 I left Rio de Janeiro, planning to travel to the Negro River, a rushed voyage after receiving a radio message from Abrão saying that our father was unwell and had fainted several times. I imagined it was a worsening of the Parkinson's disease that had been slowly debilitating him. It was a year and a half since I had last seen him, and Abrão's news left me shaken.

Even in a hurry, there is no means to travel from Rio to the Negro River in less than two days. The flight, now quicker than it was in 1986, lasts five hours, with one connection in Brasilia. The plane arrives in Porto Velho after midnight, leaving no time to catch the last coach to Guajará-Mirim. This time, as always, I took a taxi to the Hotel Central, where

I am well known to the management and staff, having stayed there for at least two decades. Then breakfast (I like the cakes there), the bus station, and a five-hour trip to Guajará, where Preta or her daughter Rafa always awaits me.

At the Hotel Mini Estrela in Guajará, I am just as well known, having now stayed there for the past thirty years. The owner of the hotel and her daughters know my favorite rooms (sixteen and seventeen), and as soon as I arrive, they ask about my two boys. The rooms are large with a ceramic tile floor, two or three single beds and a double bed in the same room, air conditioning, a bathroom, and a television. My boys always loved these enormous rooms where the three of us stayed on arriving in the city or returning from the village. I remember the time when I returned with André sick, and the relief I felt to have a bathroom and air conditioning, as well as ready access to Gil, my doctor friend, who lives nearby. On this day, when I came back from a trip to the store to buy the antibiotics prescribed by Gil, I found the room full of our Wari' friends who were in the city, sharing the beds with my kids and watching television. On another stay, at the insistence of the Wari', who admired my younger son's sophisticated taste, I had the arm of a roast monkey brought back from the village. To keep the meat dry and prevent putrefaction, I decided to try imitating the Wari' barbecue grill. I asked the cleaner, then a Bolivian woman (we were on the border with Bolivia), as tactfully as possible, with various explanations, to put the arm in the oven for me for a while. To my complete surprise, rather than being startled by the sight of the monkey arm, she looked down hungrily and exclaimed: *A mi también me gustan los monos* (I like monkeys too).

The owner of the hotel, Mercedes, and sometimes the cleaner, would lend me their bicycles during the day since it was the most common means of transport in the city. Back in 1986, when Brazil was still a long way from having cycle lanes in its city streets, Guajará had its own, an entire road dedicated to bicycles, that traversed the city from end to end, terminating at the main port of the Mamoré River where the crossing to Bolivia was made and where the city museum was situated.

I have always liked this city, which is known as the "Pearl of the Mamoré," with its tree-lined streets and many squares. Its museum on the river shore displays everything from newspapers from the period of armed conflicts between the rubber tappers and the Wari', to examples of wildlife, especially strange or defective specimens, like fetuses with two heads. In the period before Christmas 2015, the city was covered with holiday strings of colored lights that outlined the profiles of animals like reindeer and bears, right in the heart of Amazonia. Outages are still common, though not as frequent as in 1986, when there were still no electrical mainstations and the entire city was powered by generators. Right next to the museum is the customs house, where the baggage of those arriving in boats from Bolivia is searched. Each of these boats, the country's flag flying from their mast, holds around twenty people. The opposite journey, from Brazil to Bolivia, can only be made by Brazilian boats, which are exactly the same but flying the Brazilian flag. Thus the boats arrive full and leave empty on a crossing that lasts no more than fifteen minutes, traversing the Mamoré River and linking Guajará-Mirim to its Bolivian sister town, Guayaramerín.

"Jaguar-phone" in Guajará-Mirim

After two days in Guajará, everything was ready for the trip to the Negro River: gasoline for the motorboat and groceries. I awoke very early, and as soon as I opened the door of room sixteen of the Mini Estrela Hotel, I found Abrão waiting outside, ready to tell me that he had arrived overnight with our father and that he was feeling well. In fact, the entire family had traveled downriver to the city, planning to travel to Ribeirão village, accessed via the BR 364 highway and local roads. Ribeirão was set to host the Bible conference, a twice-yearly event organized by the missionaries from the New Tribes Mission, now Earth360 (its local branch known as Missão Novas Tribos do Brasil), which attracts an enormous contingent of people coming from different Wari' villages.

I packed up the food I had bought for the trip, called a taxi, and went to meet Paletó, who was already waiting for me. The house where they were all staying belonged to a local pastor. Three years earlier he had granted use of a room to two of Abrão's teenage sons, Jardison and Jackson, who went to school in the city. Far from the city center, the brick house was big, with an iron gateway that opened onto a yard and a veranda that encircled the interior of the house. During the days before we traveled to the conference, the sizeable group occupied two rooms: in addition to the two boys, there were Paletó and To'o; Abrão and his wife, Tem Xao; my namesake Aparecida, Abrão's daughter, her husband, and their small daughter, Tokohwet; as well as various other children and adolescents. The room in which Paletó and To'o were sleeping was ample but extremely hot, especially due to the corrugated fiber cement roof that covered the entire house. It had two beds, lots of clothes scattered everywhere, and a television, which was showing a *Robocop* film when I arrived. Windowless, the room had a door that opened onto the veranda and the yard. It was so hot, Paletó and To'o spent almost the whole day lying on the red cement floor of the veranda, catching the occasional breeze. It was there that I spent my last days with him.

I found Paletó more debilitated this last time. His joints were so stiff that he could not remove his shorts, unable to bend his knees. On seeing me, he began to cry and speak in the melody of the funeral song. He repeated that I was his true daughter and that he was very weak and limp, saying he was no longer the same person. He spent a lot of time with his eyes closed, as though asleep, and took some time to reply to whatever I asked him. Now and then he would cry again.

I took two small films on my tablet for him to watch. In each of the films one of my sons addressed him in Wari', calling him grandfather and saying that they were thinking of him. They had always been very close and when his strength began to fail, Paletó asked me on the phone to bring Francisco and André to say farewell to him. He said that the boys should continue my work among the Wari', but in a singular form: Francisco would be a pastor, and André, a deacon. It was To'o, his wife, who took the tablet from his hands and began to talk to the boys, as though they were there in person. "André, André, it's me, your grandmother. I'm old, I'm weak. I can no longer see well. Francisco, Francisco!" When Paletó held the tablet, he just said to one of them: "When you come here, I will no longer exist."

After this, they told me their news: who had married, who had died, the children who had been born. We all sat together on the floor of the veranda, very close to one another, with the children milling around. I had brought various foods for them that they considered delicacies, like dried fruits and granola. On each trip back and forth to the city by bike, I picked up chicken, fish, and juices, and helped one of their granddaughters prepare their meals. When I was absent for longer than usual, Paletó would anxiously await my arrival, saying that he feared I had been run over. To'o seemed very thin and dispirited to me at this time. Only later did I learn that she had tuberculosis, which would lead to her death less than a year later.

As everyone was getting ready to take a hired pickup truck to attend the Bible conference in Ribeirão, a journey that would be arduous for the two elders, I volunteered to take them in a car, which I borrowed from Funai in exchange for fuel. It was a memorable day, beginning with breakfast in the city market with manioc cake and milk cake at the stall of an acquaintance of my friend Luzia. When I arrived with the car, driven by a Wari', Paletó was waiting for me at his house, sitting on a plastic chair and wearing his best shorts and shirt. He found it very difficult to put on his flip-flop sandals since his toes, widely splayed apart, did not move. I tried to buy a pair of shoes for him, or regular sandals, but I was unsuccessful on my various attempts. We lifted his feet and slipped on the sandals, therefore, so he could get in the car. To'o sat in the middle and at the other window was his grandson Jardison, who spent the entire journey watching a clip of a duo of female singers, Simone and Simaria, on his mobile phone.

There was a big crowd of Wari' at Ribeirão, and many camping tents spread out between the houses or set up on their verandas. We headed straight to the house where Abrão and his family were camped. Paletó and To'o were given chairs to sit on, and soon people began to arrive to greet them and offer them something to eat. I had taken cakes, sandwiches, and water, which were quickly consumed. It was the conference lunch interval, and, in the distance, an enormous queue of people could be seen with plates and mugs in their hands, waiting to be served by the cooks posed behind large aluminum pans.

Paletó expressed his interest in visiting the missionary couple, Valmir and Fátima, who live there. Their house was somewhat far, in light of Paletó's mobility constraints, and our driver had left with the car to go fishing. But given the abundance of motorbikes in the village, I asked two men to take them; each sat on a pillion between the rider and someone else to support their back. And so they went, and I followed on foot. In the bustling house was not only the couple but other missionaries too, among them Teresa, who had lived on the Negro River for years and knew them both well. We sat on a sofa and chairs, and talked in Wari', a language well known to the missionaries, who worked on the translation of the Bible's books into Wari'. They told each other news, sang hymns, and finally prayed holding hands.

From there we went to the church, which was right next door, and where people headed after lunch. There they decided to seat Paletó and To'o side by side on a bench right in front of the pulpit, facing the aisle. They gave Paletó the microphone and he sang hymns. Afterwards, a queue was organized with each person approaching them one by one, shaking their hands in Western style (very lightly, the kind of handshake customarily given in the interior of Brazil) and saying something in their ears in a low voice. Orowao and A'ain Tot, their daughters, waited for their own turn in the queue, weeping, as well as Tokohwet, granddaughter, Orowao's daughter. As they approached, they hugged them and wept more intensely. When the queue was over, hymns were sung and Paletó and To'o were taken outside the church, where it was unbearably hot, and back to the house, where we waited for the car to arrive to take us back to the city.

Scattered throughout the village, the many young people and children met in groups according to age and, as in an open-air school, listened to sermons by the missionaries or other Wari'. These sermons were based around Bible stories but were also moral lectures. Some youths, detached from the groups, played with their mobiles and an app called "Bible Show," which measures the Biblical knowledge of the player via multiple-choice questions and answers, with correct responses allowing them to pass to the next phase: "What side did Jesus sit on when he went to heaven? ( ) right ( ) left ( ) above ( ) below"; or "According to Matthew 6:6, when we pray in secret, God . . . ( ) Will abhor us ( ) Will reward us ( ) Will not listen to us ( ) Will show us mercy."

I remember that on the journey back alone with Paletó, To'o, and Abílio, the Wari' driver, we talked a lot about questions of language use. The driver, himself from the OroMon territorial group like To'o, asked her about some words that today have fallen into disuse and been substituted by others. He and I chatted at length about the use of the term *parente* (kin) in Portuguese, common as a vocative for any Indigenous person in encounters involving different ethnic groups. All Indigenous people are called *parentes*, while the Whites are called by their personal name and referred to as non-Indigenous. I wanted to know how the Wari' would translate this term into their language. Indeed, as Abílio confirmed, the meaning is quite different from the Portuguese, in which *parente* generally refers to someone with whom one has genealogical relations, what we call blood relations. Among the Wari', and I am sure among many other Indigenous peoples too, the term *parente* in Portuguese serves precisely to refer to non-kin, to those for whom no kinship terms exist. In a conference in Ji-Paraná, I heard a young man from the Gavião Indigenous people begin his discourse as follows: "Good morning, kin [*parentes*]! Firstly I wish to thank God." We were unable to find an equivalent term since even the Wari' from other territorial groups, called *tatirim*, "strangers," do not fit this classification, given that an attempt will always be made to trace true kinship relations with them—something that is always possible due to the many marriages between people from different territorial groups. The question remained unresolved.

When we arrived in the city, already evening, after nearly a two-hour journey, we stopped at a little store to buy one of the last roast chickens available, accompanied by toasted manioc flour, for their dinner. The next day would be our farewell, with their voyage back to the village, in the small boat of Paulo, the husband of my sister Main. Early morning at the port, I learned that Main could not travel without first weighing and measuring her children at a health post, to ensure she would still receive her "Bolsa Família" (Family Allowance). I returned mid-afternoon and discovered that Main and her husband had already left on the boat, accompanied by their children and To'o. Paletó had stayed.

Paletó and Me, 2012

The large barge of his nephew Awo Kamip, the pastor, seemed to me the most suitable boat to take him, and I negotiated with the owner to include this new passenger in exchange for gasoline. I then went to fetch Paletó from his house, accompanied by his granddaughter, who had stayed behind to look after him. I settled him in a hammock hung up inside the boat, and put another roast chicken in his hands for him to eat on the journey. I was unable to leave the boat, fearing it would be the last time I saw him. Indeed, it was. Abrão, seeing my agony, told me what I should say to him: "I'm going now; I'll let you go."

ACKNOWLEDGMENTS

My thanks to my first readers: André Vilaça, Beatriz Albernaz, Beto Barcellos, Carlos Fausto, Claudia Fares, Daniel Willmer, Fabienne Wateau, and Francisco Vilaça. To Rafael Cariello and the journal *piauí*. To Flávio Moura and the *Todavia* publishing house for taking such good care of the original book. To those who encouraged its publication in English: João Biehl, Pedro Meira Monteiro, Tanya Luhrmann, and very especially Kate Wahl, for her welcoming enthusiasm and openness. To David Rodgers for another careful translation of my work. To the Wari', always.

My stays among the Wari' were supported by the institution where I work, the PPGAS/Museu Nacional at the Universidade Federal do Rio de Janeiro, as well as by the Funai office of Guajará-Mirim and by the funding agencies CNPQ, FAPERJ, CAPES, the Wenner-Gren Foundation, and the John Simon Guggenheim Foundation.